LOOKING IN THE PAST

Cover Image: Landscape of flowing down limestone-rich thermal water forming unusual terraces in Pamukkale (cotton castle), Southwestern Turkey

LOOKING IN THE PAST

KESHRA SANGWAL

First Edition: 2023
ISBN:

Published by Sunil Sangwal
sunil.sangwal@gmail.com

To
those who are
no more with me

CONTENTS

PREFACE

THERE ARE SEVERAL PEOPLE who write regularly important events of their lives in the form of diaries and based on these written records, some of them even publish them later. I never noted different events in my life in the form of a diary. However, somewhere in late nineteen nineties I thought that individual episodes that I heard from my elders and that I myself witnessed could serve as a record of changing traditions, mutual relationship and general life of the people in our society with time. Relying entirely on my memory I constructed some of those episodes in the form of twenty short stories and essays in the compilation *Excursions in Past and Present*, which were published two years ago.

This compilation of six stories and one essay is my recollection of periods of events and observations as a school boy, a research student, a post-doctoral fellow, an academic teacher, a visitor, and a witness of the society. Characters and events in a chapter are based on their sequential description over a specific period. Each chapter is a narration of strong and weak sides of human behaviour. Most of the characters involved in the events of different narrations are real. Therefore, if someone of these characters feels offended by the way I describe the events in which he/she participates, my sincere apologies in advance.

Keshra Sangwal
April 2023

1

MY SIXTH CLASS

MY DAYS OF CHILDHOOD were wonderful in different ways. Irrespective of whether I came across an uncle, an aunt, a cousin or elder siblings, all were generous and affectionate. I do not remember that I ever heard harsh words as a child. When I made some mistake or mischief, they considered it natural for me to do in the days of childhood. With age I was deprived of all concessions of childhood, and slowly I began to adopt the rules governing the society. However, I realize now that my adjacency with the elders in the days of my childhood was an interesting laboratory for my observation of things happening in the surroundings.

I came to know new names and new happenings during conversations of my father and his uncles with their visitors. I heard description like 'Bhiráj's' for "Bhiráj's sons" instead of giving names of the sons of uncle Bhiráj, who was older than my father by several years. Other names that I heard were: Shoji, Shoráj, Jekisan, Jerám, Kisan, Dirám, among others, for Shivaji, Shivaráj, Jaikrishan, Jairám, Krishan, and Dayárám. In our neighbouring village many names were similar to those in ours, but there were also unusual names like Kaptán, Dipati and Laftain in a family, derived from Captain, Deputy and Lieutenant. It was rumoured that during a Police enquiry in a particular case in this neighbouring village, these persons were witnesses and were asked to introduce themselves. When they gave their names, the Police Inspector observed that the entire army was there. The point is that this type of narration and

1

distorted names was common in our villages in those days. Names of Hindu Gods, Ráma and Krishna, usually followed the names of males in our village simply as a token of their remembrance, but the suffix "Singh" followed the names in the neighbouring village as an indication of believers of the Sikh faith.

In the days of my childhood dusty winds blowing un-interruptedly for several days and long periods of failure in water supply in our canals were common in summer. Village life was the ultimate sufferer of both of these elements. Though drinking water from some of the wells dug outside the village could have somewhat soothed the daily nervousness of villagers, sour water in these wells was unfit for drinking. Insufficient irrigation of agricultural fields resulting in poor crops was another steady source of their nervousness. Rain pour in monsoon season was the only relief for somewhat longer periods when villagers could store water in ponds full to their brim in the out-skirts of their villages. In view of large families and limited sources of income to support them it was a general tendency in those days to owe new fields situated not far away from our villages for cultivation in nearby regions of other states, where their irrigation by existing, and possibly new, canals was anticipated in future. Sarhadi canal running down south close to the newly created Pákistán border was the hope of future for the irrigation of barren fields in the old Srigangánagar district of Rájasthán. These fields had been measured and organized in units called "chaks" clustered around a town or city, known as tehsil, as their administrative headquarter.

Names of the chaks in the south of Srigangánagar were distinguished from each other by combining two capital letters of the English alphabet preceded by one Arabic numeral. For example, close to the city of Srigangánagar, some of the chaks are 2ML, 3ML or 5ML and a canal passed through these chaks. Usually, residents of these chaks called them by using Hindi word for the Arabic numeral followed by phonetic sounds of letters of the English alphabet, for example, do-em-el, teen-em-el, etc., but some of them were also known by the name of individual persons and family surnames.

At the time of independence Srigangánagar was a small town with scattered houses built mainly from sun-baked mud bricks, and was connected to other known cities like Hanumángarh Junction, Bikáner and the state capital Jaipur by narrow-gauge railway track. Elder people in our region knew the city by its old name of Rámnagar, but the younger generation slowly began to replace this name by Gangánagar, a diminutive form of the official name of Srigangánagar in commemoration of Mahárájá Gangá Singh. In fact, most of the surviving people of those days still call the city by this diminutive form. Roads connecting this city with other main towns were built mainly after the independence, but bus transport was rare in view of small number of bus routes allotted by the administration and harsh climate prevailing in the region.

From the Srigangánagar railway station chaks 2ML, 3ML or 5ML were 4 to 5 km away. When I was a young child, man-driven rickshaws served as an easy mode of transport of passengers between these chaks and the city bazaar. Somewhat later horse-driven two-wheel carriages began to carry local passengers, but relatively faster diesel-engine driven three-wheelers, connecting even distantly situated villages, slowly replaced them. Long-route buses, which were not many then, preferred to earn as much as they could by carrying long-distant passengers, and prospective passengers from these chaks had to curse their fate when they could not manage to catch some other mode of transport to travel to the city despite hours of patience at the bus-stand. Buses carrying passengers even on their roof-tops were common features of those days.

When a primary school sanctioned by the Punjáb Government after independence began to function in 1956 in its building erected by the joint efforts and resources of our village, the main task of the only teacher responsible for the school was to enrol students for different classes from the children of the village. He enrolled new students for the first class and qualified some other children taught before privately by different teachers for higher classes. However, after assessing my knowledge, he informed my father that I knew more than that required for admission in the fifth class, and advised that I should be admitted somewhere else in a middle or high school.

The advice of the teacher-in-charge of the school, combined with my desire to continue education, motivated my father and elder brothers to send me to Gangánagar to have my schooling there. The choice was made from consideration of my boarding with a distant uncle living there and accessibility of education in a high school with the brother of my cousin sister's husband as its headmaster. They also took into account my occasional visit to my father's younger sister, Rukmani, traditionally known in our family by her abridged name 'Rukmá', who lived with her two sons in 3ML Chak near this city. This aunt owned 25 beeghás (about 16 acres) of agricultural land purchased earlier by her late husband's parents from government administration which planned the sale of the land of the Chak to the public. Her late in-laws were the residents of Killánwáli before. This village is not far away from our village. Apart from the above factors, it was possible to reach Gangánagar by train from Sádulshahar, popularly known as 'Matilee' in those days. Probably this name was derived from heaps of sand encountered in its vicinity while reaching there during summer. This small town is some 10 miles away to the south from our village. In those days one could reach Sádulshahar either on foot or on camel-back when one carried heavy luggage for the onward journey. It was the beginning of planning and construction, by Public Works Department, of an asphalted road-way joining Abohar with Hanumángarh.

My aunt's elder son, Rámchandra, worked as a Patwári and was a widower. He had a son from his late wife. Most of the time he was on duty in his area of services and occasionally used to come home. The younger son, Doongar, looked after the fields. He was married and had a son. The aunt mainly stayed at home, looked after the elder grandson, cradled the younger grandson, and took care of a few cows and buffaloes for milk and milk products for home consumption.

The uncle with whom I was to stay in Gangánagar was older than my father by several years and was distantly related to our family through his mother. For this reason my father used to call him "Dirámbhái" but I always addressed him "Táyooji" (Big Uncle). He lived with his only son, Bahádur, in a two-room house with spacious courtyard and entrance to the north from the street in the older part of the city popularly known as "Puráni Ábádee." The street ended after a couple of houses beyond uncle's house and

bifurcated thereby restricting the spreading of the locality
to the west. From the end of the street one could easily
see a large then-defunct red-coloured construction of the
regional administration, known as "Old Tehsil", and vast
empty space around it, which served as a playground for
volleyball and football lovers. Like most of the houses
in this part, the uncle's house was built from sun-baked
mud bricks. An exception was the Old Tehsil, built from
kiln-baked bricks, to the west of the uncle's house.

The uncle hailed from a remote village south of Gangánagar, where his family had a piece of land. Yearly yield of
crops like barley, chickpea and mustard rested entirely on
the whims of monsoon season. When he was still young,
his parents expired and he was left with his wife and a
younger brother. After the death of his parents, he arranged his brother's marriage and he himself was blessed
with a son. However, some time later an epidemic occurred
in the area, when many people, including the uncle's wife,
died in the village. Keeping in mind more possible casual-
ties in the village due to the epidemic and the tough time
ahead in raising his son there, the uncle decided to leave
the ancestral property to his younger brother and to raise
and educate his son, Bahádur, in Gangánagar. Thus, with
his son he shifted to the city, took odd jobs, purchased
a plot of land to construct a house, sent his son to the
government school for education, and cooked food on a
home-made hearth by burning dried logs of cotton-plants
for the two in rudimentary conditions of those days. With
the passage of time, the uncle built a liveable house, and
his son completed his high school education from Government High School and obtained the job of an inspector in
a Cooperative Bank in the city.

In Gangánagar there were three high schools in those days. The first was the Government High School, mentioned above, with negligible tuition fee per month for its students, and two privately managed high schools: Mahárishi Dayánand High School and Biháni High School, where the tuition fee was somewhat higher than that in the Government High School, which not all could afford in those days. Government High School was situated on the west of the only narrow canal flowing between the railway station and the Puráni Ábádee, Biháni High School on the southern periphery of the city on the Hanumángarh Road, whereas Mahárishi Dayánand High School was located in the interior of the city.

When I began to live with the uncle, I saw my cousin brother Bahadur, whom I always addressed as Bháiji, going to his bank early in the morning after taking an early bath and a quick breakfast. This was also the time for me to go to my school, Mahárishi Dayánand High School, situated close to Anáj Mandi (Grain Market). This school was to the east of the uncle's house at a distance of about 4 kilometres beyond the narrow canal, popularly known as 'Kuttá Liknee' (literally: sipper for dogs), which was roughly halfway between the school and the uncle's house. The name Kuttá Liknee was perhaps given to this canal because one could frequently see stray dogs swimming in it in the hot months of summer. Walking home from the school after my lessons in the summer was an everyday experiment when I had to stop a couple of times under the shadows of trees alongside the road to heave a sigh of relief from the heat pouring from above.

I was not enrolled formally in the school, but I was officially permitted to attend lessons for 6th class students, thanks to the permission from the school headmaster. I used to sit on a bench somewhere in fourth or fifth row in the middle column of benches arranged in three columns from the teachers' table. One of the students sitting on my bench was from a family which had come from Uttar Pradesh. His father was employed in some factory in the city to maintain the functioning of diesel engines to run factory machines.

Táyooji was always dressed in a while dhoti tied around his loin and a collared shirt covering it up to the thighs. He usually purchased a pair of white dhotis and placed an order to his tailor to sew a shirt for him according to measurement from the cloth he had purchased before in the market. He was happy with wearing one set of dhoti and shirt and keeping another set washed by him at home to replace the one he wore after a bath. He also used a piece of white pure cotton cloth which served both as a turban to cover his head and a towel to wipe sweat in summer days.

Táyooji had a precisely defined schedule for his daily life. He used to get up early in the morning much before dawn and take a bath in cold water with his dhoti wrapped around the loin. Then he used to replace it with another dry dhoti, and spread the wet dhoti on a long cotton string tied to two nails fixed in nearby walls of the house. After his bath of the morning he used to sing his áratees and bhajans loudly in praise of different deities in his room. Thereafter he cooked food for the three of us and when my cousin brother and I had left home, he went out for walk and to meet his friends, and when we returned he was always at home. After taking lunch, which we usually called 'dopahariyá', I kept myself busy with doing my homework from the school and my cousin went through a newspaper in Hindi, which he usually bought on his way back from his office, and did some pending work in the files that he had brought from his office. During these hours Táyooji rested in his chárpayee with occasional naps. He was content with the news that he heard from his friends and his son, and never behaved as a news-monger or a man of great wisdom. In the evening he cooked food for us, had his supper after saying his evening prayers, and went to bed when he felt that it was already night.

Táyooji never used any clock when he would go to bed at night or to wake up in the morning. It was his biological clock that regulated his daily way of life and his intuitive knowledge of the world around him. It is true that Táyooji did not have other option than his reliance on Nature because he never went to any school. He was happy that, thanks to his consistent efforts over years, his son was educated and was an inspector in the Cooperative Bank. But I did hear occasional brief exchange of words of discord between the father-son duo over some issues which remained incomprehensible to me at that time.

Occasionally, in the evenings I went out for short strolls in the locality. I found that the headmaster of our school lived at the end of the nearly side street to the east of the our main street. His house had its main entrance from the east in the form of a Persian-style darwázá. While strolling in the Old Tehsil area and beyond, I usually happened to see some tall young men from the locality playing volleyball. I knew that they were from the locality because I had seen some of them sitting on chárpáyees resting on the chowkees before their houses on the street to my school. I was enormously impressed by the services and volleys by some of them. From their games I imagined that they were perhaps the best and could defeat all teams, although I did not see before another team playing volleyball. It was exciting to see them wearing undershirts drenched with sweat and wiping their sweat off their forehead time and again.

I was always overjoyed to see aunt Rukmá or her younger son, Doongar, visiting us with small "Dáldá-brand" cans containing ghee obtained by churning milk-curd at home. The aunt showered affection on all of us. She considered Táyooji as her elder brother and cousin Bahádur as her own nephew, and both of them were indeed fond of her. When I had a couple of holidays in the school, I tried to visit the aunt by riding a man-driven rickshaw from the end of the Anáj Mandi, but this feat required reaching there from Táyooji house and back on foot. This was tiresome for an 11-year old boy like me, but stay with the aunt was a great reward.

After the rainy season when day-time temperature began to recede, I saw kiln-baked bricks being piled up in the courtyard of the uncle's house and inauguration of the construction of a drawing room and an adjoining main entrance to the house along the street. When this construction work came to an end, a new kitchen, a bathroom and other necessary amenities were added to the house. Some time later I learned that a date has been fixed for the marriage of cousin Bahádur. His would-be bride was the niece of one the volleyball players I had seen before in the playground close to Old Tehsil. He was a school teacher. His would-be father-in-law, Jeevan Singh, was a government official, who had a house adjoining his brother's on the east of the same street. I heard that these brothers originally came from Patti Billa village in Punjáb, not far away from Gangánagar. They had settled here long ago when they were young, received their education and later got jobs according to their qualifications. Their eldest brother still lived in Patti and looked after the ancestral property.

When the day of marriage of cousin Bahádur approached, guests poured in from far and near to attend the wedding ceremony, with aunt Rukmá as the lady supervising it in the house. Following the traditions of those days, the cousin was first dressed elegantly as bridegroom and rode a decorated horse, with me sitting behind him on the horse-back as his younger brother and the marriage-party following the bridegroom on the horse, to the bride's house. After the marriage ceremony the bride reached her destined house as my bhábhee (brother's wife; sister-in-law) and its first lady resident since Táyooji began to live with his son here. At the time of her entrance to her husband's house she was accompanied, among others, by her younger school-going brother, Raghuveer. He was somewhat younger to me, but after the marriage whenever we met each other, we enjoyed spending time together. However, after the arrival of Bhábhee Táyooji began to live mainly in the newly-built drawing room where I too took refuge when some ladies came to see Bhábhee. The drawing room also served to entertain different male guests occasionally visiting the family, with me as the waiter-at-hand for the family. I considered it a distinction. However, then I felt more frequent loud discussions between Táyooji and Bahádurbhái and increased nervousness in Táyooji behaviour.

It was the beginning of spring season that I came to know in the school that nayá or new paisá based on decimal system of the Indian currency was going to substitute the old áná-paisá system. According to this new system, 100 nayá paisas were to replace 64 paisá, with 4 paisás for one áná, and 16 ánás for 1 rupee. We were somewhat baffled with this change for some time, but slowly common man forgot the ánás completely and became accustomed to the nayá paisá which ultimately began to be known as paisá of the day. It was 1957 when nayá paisá came into being and cousin Bahádur's marriage was solemnized.

When the academic year was about to end, I was told that Biháni High School was the centre of my examinations of different subjects taught during the year and that after passing the subjects I would receive my passing certificate which would enable me for admission in the seventh class. The reason of having examinations in Biháni High School was the fact that I was a private student unlike my classmates who were regular students of the Mahárishi Dayánand High School.

Before the dates of examinations we had some free days for preparation of syllabi taught to us from textbooks that we had purchased in the beginning of the year and from classroom notes in our notebooks. Later, despite the difficult task of walking miles of distance for me as a child to and from the examination centre, I took written examinations of different subjects following the notified schedule.

Checking of our answer-sheets by appropriate examiners was a time-consuming process, which caused declaration of results of examinations after some time. In my case the situation was not different. It was wheat harvesting season at that time when even delicate hands of young boys like mine were considered helpful. My aunt Rukmá had told my father before that she wanted me to stay with her family after the completion of the year to help in harvesting and threshing their wheat crop. Therefore, after the examinations I left for 3ML Chak to be of some use to the aunt's family.

The conventional way of trampling out wheat and barley grains from the gathered crop in those days was to spread it around an empty circular space of appropriate radius and then to crush the mass in installments by an assembly of acacia branches pulled by a pair of bullocks or a camel walking in circular motion. The empty circular space was kept to collect parts of crushed mass of the crop containing the grain. The pair of bullocks was goaded by an adult man walking between them and the assembly of acacia branches, but the camel was usually driven by a young child riding on its back. Since walking for long duration was difficult, the responsibility of goading bullocks was frequently shared by two or more adults but a child could ride a camel for hours uninterruptedly. Exception was the period of some hottest 3-4 hours of the noon for rest when farming community gave some fodder to their animals, boiled tea with milk on a provisional hearth, took dopahariyá, and had a nap after the food. The choice between bullocks and camels for trampling out wheat grains was entirely a matter of what a farming family owned.

On arrival at aunt's house I found that chickpea and mustard crops grown in the fields had already been harvested and wheat crop had been cut and gathered at one place for trampling out its grain. Since the aunt's family owned a camel, it was this camel that they could use for trampling of wheat grain with me as the right person to ride their camel. In those days aunt's younger son, Doongar, was responsible for the task of cultivation of fields and harvesting of crops. He was guided in this endeavour by aunt Rukmá and her elder son, Rámchandra. Therefore, brother Doongar took me under his wings and I began to ride the camel for trampling of wheat grain following the traditional working schedule.

We used to come to work after taking a small breakfast well before dawn when it was still not so hot and began to thresh wheat under the assembly of acacia branches pulled by the camel. We continued this work until Doongarbhái's wife, my another bhábhee, came with food and skimmed milk for us, which she always carried in a basket on her head. After a short break to take food, we continued our work until the sunlight was still withstandable when we set out for the noonrest for a couple of hours. After the noonrest we continued our work practically up to the sunset. When the process of trampling was finished, it was time to separate grain from the crushed mass by blowing it manually in a natural stream of wind using special wooden implements with four- or five-pronged forks fixed to handles. It was a luxury to have uniform flow of wind for this purpose at this stage of trampling in which all tried to participate. Finally, after the separation of wheat grain from the crushed mass, Doongarbhái carried the grain and the crushed grain-free mass of wheat plants, popularly known as turhee, in his camel-driven cart to his house.

After the completion of the harvest season I stayed with the aunt for some days. When results of my examination were announced, Bahádurbhái collected my passing certificate from the Education Department. Equipped with the certificate, I left for home by catching a train to Sádul-shahar first and then from there by walking on foot to the village.

My problem of admission in the seventh class did not end with the possession of passing certificate. Government Middle School of the adjoining village, Rámsará, declined to recognize my certificate because it was not issued from a school in Punjáb. Therefore, my family decided to get me admitted in Government High School in Sádulshahar, and made arrangements of my lodging with a family in which a daughter of our village was married and boarding with a dhábá situated close to the railway station to its south and an array of offices of commission agents to its north.

Some years later I was saddened to hear the news that Dirám Táyooji left his house over some petty issue and began the life of a wanderer staying at different places and with different people for short duration. He expired in a takiyá (residence of a sádhu on the outskirts of a village), where some sádhus performed his last funeral rites.

January 2022

2

WHEN I ACQUIRED HIGHER EDUCATION

I ALWAYS HAD PROBLEM WITH memorizing contents of fragments of textbooks of courses of studies since the days of my childhood. Instead I tried to understand the gist of the contents and faithfully describe them, whenever necessary, in my own words in the classroom or in the examination. However, early in the school days I recognized that this approach was not sufficient, especially, in the case of subjects like history and geography where one was required to remember not only events but also their years and precise data or facts. It was always an uphill task for me to remember the administrative or agricultural reforms introduced by different kings and emperors in the country during their rules. Based on somewhat general trends of reforms by every ruler in every duration my round-about way of describing the reforms in the answer-books of examination of history in the school levels enabled my promotion to the next class on my own with very low scores and, when the scores were too low, my teachers were always generous enough to promote me to the next class. In those days I envied my class-fellows who achieved high scores in the examination of these subjects by writing down answers to the questions from the memorized portions of prescribed textbooks.

The problem of my incapability of memorizing texts haunted me even in later years of my education. In my BSc

17

examination in 1965 I managed well with mathematics, but my scores in chemistry and physics were simply acceptable. The consequence of this outcome of examinations was difficulty in getting admission for studies for MSc degree. My colleagues, dependent on writing down memorized materials from the curricula, again happened to be better than me and were admitted comfortably for higher education in institutions in the State or outside it. The result of my intellectual deficiency of memorizing material was that, after obtaining my BSc degree, I had to wait for one year to be enrolled for my MSc degree in physics in a relatively newly established university in Vallabh Vidyánagar in the State of Gujarát more than a thousand kilometres away from home. This university, Sardár Patel University, had previously been working for some two decades as Sardár Vallabhbhái Vidyápeeth. Mr Bhatti, who was a demonstrator of physics practicals in our college when we were doing our BSc in early sixties, served as a guide in this endeavour. He had completed his MSc in this University in the previous year. Sushil Dhawan, who did his BSc with me and had scores similar to mine, was also admitted there with Mr Bhatti's guidance. Following instructions received from the University we duly remitted tuition and hostel fees using services of Post and Telegraph Department, as it was called in those days, and prepared for the journey to our University by train in the beginning of June 1966.

Travel to the University of our admission by train was a three-stage matter. First we had to reach Old Delhi, then to Barodá, now known as Vadodará, and finally to Ánand, the nearest railway station. Those were the days when only a couple of coaches of a long-route train were reserved as sleepers and no bedsheets and blankets were provided by Indian Railways. Moreover, reservations were difficult to make on the day of departure or even a couple of days before the departure. However, touts at railways stations and coach attendants sometimes served the needy at some extra pocket money. An alternative way to travel, though less comfortably, on such occasions was to force one's way into an unreserved coach through one of its windows and occupy some seat, leaving behind the luggage with his companion on the platform. After the occupant had settled, this companion handed the entire luggage of both of them, again through the nearest window, and later joined him by squeezing his way through the crowd in one of the main gates of the coach. Travelling with ladies was highly nervous and tough under these circumstances.

In those days there was no direct fast railway train from Abohar to Delhi, but a couple of passenger trains ran between Hindumalkot, the last railway station on the West Pákistán border, and Bathindá Junction. One of these passenger trains left Abohar in the evening and reached Bathindá Junction roughly at midnight. This train had an attached coach for passengers travelling to Old Delhi. At Bathindá Junction this coach was shunted to Punjáb Mail, a fast train which reached Delhi at about seven in the morning. Punjáb Mail ran everyday between Ferozepur Cantonment and Bombay Central, following a route not on our way to our University.

With our rolled beddings and other luggage Sushil and I reached Old Delhi by boarding the coach at Abohar. At Old Delhi station we waited till about 1 PM to board one of the unreserved coaches of Janatá Express to reach Barodá next day at noon. After waiting for some two hours at the Barodá station we got into a passenger train on its way to

Ahmedabád to reach Ánand after some half an hour. Just outside the main entrance of the Ánand Railway station across the road, we availed ourselves of the local bus service to our destination, Vallabh Vidyánagar, located some 4 km away from the station. After alighting from the bus at the bus-stand of our destination we were guided by incidentally encountered people to reach Nehru Hall, the hostel of our residence, in the residential area of the University, with our rolled beddings and luggage intact.

Apart from the torment of getting into the coach of a train and getting out of it during our journey, it was a marvellous and unforgettable experience of guarding our entire luggage and money from prevalent theft and pick-pocketing in trains and of planning to satisfy our thirst and hunger during the journey. To satisfy thirst and hunger we had to wait for hours for the train to stop for longer durations at stations of big cities like Ratlám, where we could drink cold water from taps, buy cups of tea in small earthen pots, called kullarhs, and buy food items like freshly-cooked loaves or deep-fried purees, with some spiced cooked chickpeas or seasonal vegetable atop them, all on a banyan leaf or a piece of local newspaper.

The residential area of the University contained three or four rows of quarters for lecturers and readers on the north, one row of quarters for professors on the south, several scattered quarters for administrative staff on the east, a cluster of quarters for researchers on the south east and Nehru Hall, the hostel for MSc and PhD male students, in its neighbourhood on the south-west; all of them were well connected and separated by asphalted roads. University administration and post-graduate departments were situated to the west of the residential area at a distance of about one km. When we walked to the university administration from our hostel, we first came across large private houses, then a small market and, finally beyond the market, a long straight asphalted road connected to Karamsad Road to the south, but to the north this road underwent a curvature to the west. Beyond this road to its west lay a big playground surrounded by different undergraduate colleges and hostels for their male students, and to the north there were a ladies hostel, medical centre, College of Education, postgraduate departments, university library and university administration. The ladies hostel and the College of Education had their entrances to the outer asphalted road, which crossed another road, running perpendicular to it, after passing by Department of Physics next to the College of Education. The Department of Physics had its main entrance from the perpendicular road, which went to Bákrol village to the north, but one could also enter it from the north by walking on the narrow passage between the hedges surrounding it. Department of Chemistry functioned just opposite to the Department of Physics, on the other side of the perpendicular road, but it had its main entrance to the north on the outer road. Residence of the Vice-Chancellor of the University was situated to the north of the Department of Physics, across the road before the road to Bákrol.

Nehru Hall was a four-storeyed building, ground floor and three more floors above it, and had two wings, with doors of the rooms on either sides of long corridors. We were allotted a room on the first floor of the left wing. This two-segment room had a large segment as living and reading space and another narrow outer segment, on the roadside, which served us as free space to prepare tea, store drinking water in a pitcher, keep various necessary utensils and spread on a string our wet clothes to dry after bathing and washing. Entrance to the room had a large cupboard and open shelves adjoining it and the empty space above them had the construction of rectangular boxes of depth of the cupboard. We spread our beddings on the two bare beds in the inner segment, rested our other luggage in the cupboards, and the empty tin suitcases in the shelves. Common toilets and bath rooms, situated at the end of each wing, were separated from the two rows of rooms by bridge-like structures.

We came to know that, in the hostel, there was a mess where we could have, on monthly basis, two meals: an early lunch and a supper, but arrangement of breakfast we had to make ourselves. We managed to acquire an old kerosene stove left with some senior students by previous inhabitants, a utensil for preparing tea in the morning, a pitcher for drinking water and a tumbler with a long handle to draw water to drink from the pitcher. We were also told that we could buy milk, in the morning, sold by a milk vendor from the Amul Dairy in Ánand. With this basis, Sushil and I settled in the hostel environment and began to attend our classes in the Department of Physics.

Our teaching schedule started at 10 AM and ended at 5 PM. First we had some 3-4 lectures on different subjects and then the so-called practicals related to obtaining data from experiments on some physical phenomenon in the laboratory and their subsequent analysis. Therefore, to reach the Department well before the lectures we used to take a very early lunch (precisely, a late solid breakfast) before 9:30 AM and then take our supper after our teaching schedule at about 6 PM in the hostel mess, with a short break for tea in ceramic cups on some of road-side tea stalls in the open before the practicals. Our other tea or milk that we had was in glass tumblers every morning after our routine morning baths. Desired volume of milk, sold by the Amul Dairy vendor on the road outside close to the hostel, irrespective of weather and season, in our utensil satisfied our needs. To satisfy our thirst in those summer days we drank water from the water-pot in our room and from the water cooler in the Department.

The academic staff of the Department, when we joined it, was modest. There was one professor (Ambubhái R. Patel), who was also the head of the Department, one reader (Manubhái S. Joshi) and one lecturer (Maganbhái M. Patel). The former two had obtained their PhD degrees from University College, London, under the supervision of Professor S. Tolansky, who introduced multiple-beam interferometry for the study of surfaces of single crystals. A.R. Patel received his PhD degree on the etching of diamond, whereas M.S. Joshi on the natural surfaces of quartz crystals, where they extensively used the technique of multiple-beam interferometry. The stays of both of them for their PhDs in London were financed by Chárutar Vidyá Mandal, a trust for promotion of higher education in this Chárutar region of Gujarát. Since A.R. Patel received his PhD degree earlier than M.S. Joshi, the former headed the Department because of his seniority in services. Maganbhái M. Patel did not have a PhD degree. Therefore, he was employed on the post of a lecturer. Somewhat later Shankarbhái M. Patel and Mahendra K. Agarwál, two other MSc holders, were recruited as lecturers. The first lecture was always given by Professor A.R. Patel, but there was no preference of the hour for other teachers. Practicals were supervised by Dr Joshi and the lecturers. Chandrakánt Patel was responsible for technical assistance in practical work and maintenance of the equipment for practicals, and Babubhái Chauhán looked after secretarial work and purchases of different articles required in the Department. In this work he was assisted by Prakásh Sálvi who worked mainly as a typist of various types of correspondence.

Professor Patel taught statistical physics and solid state physics, Dr Joshi taught modern physics and crystallography, and Maganbhái Patel, Shankarbhái Patel and Mahendra Agarwál taught other subjects like classical mechanics and mathematical physics. These lecturers were also carrying out research work for their PhDs under the supervision of Professor Patel. Except for Mahendra K. Agarwál, other members of the staff were from Gujarát. Agarwál hailed from Mount Ábu in Rajasthán, a popular summer resort to the north, not far way from the border with Gujarát.

The Department of Physics, at that time, was housed in a two-storeyed building, with lecture halls, laboratories for practicals and research work, rooms and offices for the academic staff and research students, department library containing research journals, store-room and administrative office, in a square structure surrounding a large compound covered with well-maintained grass. It had three entrances planned just after the northern, western and southern rows of rooms. The main entrance was located on the south after the western row of rooms. It was connected to the perpendicular road and the University administration across this road. The other two entrances were located in diagonally opposite directions on the west and east after the northern and southern rows of rooms, respectively. The eastern entrance was always kept closed and a water-cooler housed there served all in satisfying their thirst. All members of the staff traditionally used simple bicycles as a convenient mode of communication to the Department via the main southern entrance with a permanent bicycle-stand to park them behind a gate which remained open during the teaching hours. However, students coming on foot usually entered and left the Department through the western entrance because this way they had to walk a distance shorter than that from the direction of the main entrance.

Contrary to our anticipation, our batch of twenty students for first-year physics was from different states of India. Apart from Sushil and me, there was Singlá from Barnála (Punjáb), Bádám from Srinagar (Jammu and Kashmir), Bhagwati Agarwál from Mount Abu (Rájasthán), and Abraham, Benjamin, Verghese and Vilásini, among several others, from different parts of Kerala. This trend was not unique for our batch. Composition of the batch of students for the second-year physics was also similar. Among these second-year students were: Surender Dhawan and Ramesh Kálrá (Punjab), and Roop Kishen Táku (Jammu and Kashmir). In those years a majority of the students and the few female students, usually one each year, to study physics in a batch were from Kerala. In general, not many students from Gujarát opted for the study of physics, and students admitted from other states of the country than Kerala were also not abundant.

In contrast to the Department of Physics most of the students to study chemistry were from Gujarát. However, several students from outside Gujarát could be seen in the Departments of Biology, Economics and Mathematics. For example, in the first year of our studies, Ávaddán Cháran was doing his MA in Economics, and Santokh Mathároo his MSc in Statistics. Cháran was from Sirohi (Rájasthán), but he was inspired by his maternal uncle to join this University. This maternal uncle lived in Vidyánagar and owned a photostudio. Mathároo just had his roots in Punjáb but did not hail from there because his parents had settled in Ánand long ago and the entire family spoke Gujaráti. In fact, with the passage of time we came to know several research students doing their PhDs in the Department, who were not from Gujarát. The main wish to know these senior students was our poor knowledge of the Gujaráti language and the fact that Hindi was something like a lingua franca in this academic community and we felt more closeness to the people of the North in the initial stage of our stay there.

There were several so-called research scholars working for their PhDs in the Department. Professor Patel and Dr Joshi were the two recognized supervisors for PhD students, but a majority of them were registered with Professor Patel perhaps because he was senior and had more possibilities of finding scholarships for them as the Head of the Department. Among these research students O.P. Bahl and A.S. Vagh were practically finalizing their PhD theses on graphite and quartz, respectively, and K.S. Raju, Chandrakant C. Desai, M.A. Ittyachen and Pushkar N. Kotru were doing their PhDs on gypsum, fluorite, apophyllite, and quartz crystals, respectively. Then there were S.V. Deshpande and V. Damodardas, working on crystal structure determination and thin films, respectively, and R.M. Chaudhari, Rajendra P. Singh and Jacob Koshy on alkali halide, barium fluoride and barium sulphate crystals. However, in the first year of our studies, we kept ourselves aloof from these research students because of our notion that we were not wise enough to initiate a talk with them.

We organised our student life reasonably well. To achieve this we purchased some odd items needed in our daily life from shops in the small market on our way to the Department. We also keenly watched the behaviour of Kálrá and Táku, our senior colleagues, who were doing well with their studies. They were unusually friendly with us for the simple reason that Kálrá's elder brother had taught us before during our studies for the BSc degree and we could speak in Punjábi. They lived together in one of the rooms on our floor, and we frequently visited them.

The land outside the residential area of the University on our way to the Department from our hostel had been sold as residential plots with appropriately planned roads, but many of the plots were without any construction on them and the roads were also provisional. The boundaries of residences on already-built plots frequently had well-maintained hedges of jasmine shrubs. The presence of these shrubs could easily be felt from the pleasing fragrance of their white flowers while passing by them in the morning hours.

Kálrá and Táku had their own stories. Táku was a chain smoker and began his day by lighting a cigarette, but Kálrá was a non-smoker. Kálrá had a good memory. We were told that once he closed his eyes during a lecture for a sufficiently long time. The lecturer noted this and thought that Kálrá was not serious with the lecture and had fallen asleep. Therefore, he asked Kálra what the teaching was about. Kálrá stood up and reproduced all that the lecturer had taught. The lecturer thereafter continued his lesson without any comment on Kálrá's way of attendance.

Kálrá's explanation of this incidence was that there was no compulsion to see someone's face if one did not like it.

Once it occurred to the above colleagues to save time in the morning by having long and deep sleep dressed in pants and shirts at night and to go to attend lectures directly after taking the early food. To have long and pleasant dreams they took bath before going to the bed, applied talc powder on the body and went to sleep on beds decorated with fresh twigs of jasmine shrubs that they picked from the hedge of some of the residences nearby.

Kálrá had a talent to cram large portions of texts from the books he had. He told us that once he did not understand the question properly. Therefore, unsure of domain of the correct reply, he simply wrote down in the answerbook all that he had crammed on that topic and left the choice of the appropriate reply to the examiner. On the question of cramming the entire book of solid state physics he told that it could probably take him two weeks. Usually, he did not close the door of his room from inside during the day. In his room we could frequently see him lying on his bed covered with a bedsheet or a blanket forming a tent-like structure held on his folded knees. Judging from his posture a visitor understood that he was sleeping and did not dare to disturb him. But he studied in this state. Once I went to his room and did not find him neither studying nor sleeping there. Later he told that he had been studying in the empty rectangular box above the entrance door. He invented this method of studying in this box above the door using the tent-like structure on his folded knees to go unnoticed in the room. We never understood how he managed to remember long passages from books and lecture-notes, but the fact is that he obtained his MSc degree with excellent scores. Contrary to his roommate, Táku did not rely much on cramming but he too obtained his MSc with good scores.

From the life of the people and the climate in my part of Punjáb we noticed here several differences. We observed frequent rains on our arrival here in contrast to the dry climate in Punjáb. Many middle-aged and older males wore white dhoti and Gandhian cap, but in Punjáb, in this type of attire, we met occasionally male workers of the Congress Party mainly coming from Uttar Pradesh although local workers of the Congress Party usually wore khádi kurtá-pyjámá. The University Vice-Chancellor, Ishwarbhái Patel, was an example of males in this typical attire. It was common to find young and old people, even college and university teachers, wearing plastic slippers here, but people in Punjáb always wore Bátá-brand leather shoes purchased in the city or regional brand of leather shoes, called jutees, stitched by local cobblers in the villages. Young girls here, as a rule, were dressed in frocks, but in our part of Punjáb their cousins usually wore salwár-kameez. Ladies here wore sáris, but not many ladies could be seen in sárees in Punjáb. Occasionally, one could also see some elderly women with a garland of beady jasmine flowers wound around the knot of their long hair spiralled either on the back of their head or behind their right ear. In contrast to the traditional spicy two-coarse meals of Punjáb, in the hostel mess we found our two-time meals composed of baked loaves from wheat or bájari flour or boiled rice as staple food served with a liquid mixture of seasonal vegetables, lentils and beans cooked in water containing unrefined brown sugar.

We came to know that on some Sundays our hostel mess served specialized food as a substitute of two-time meals, known as feasts, containing local delicious dishes like shrikhand, rasgullás or guláb-jámuns. The biggest advantage of the feasts was that one could concentrate on eating the delicious items alone to one's satisfaction, but the disadvantage was that one had to visit some local bar in the town for evening meals. The mess contractor always fixed charges for these feasts for individual visitors much higher than the cost of two-time meals. The feasts were indeed opportunities for the mess contractor to earn money from outsiders. These feasts were quite popular with the local students and many of them indeed waited for them. Occasionally, the students residing in the hostel invited guests to relish the feasts despite their high charges. Perhaps the inviting student knew beforehand that his guest would do justice to the invitation by consuming appropriate mass of the specialized food of the feast.

A couple of months after our arrival we began to hear chorus singing dominated by female voices somewhere nearby in the colony. The singing was heard after the night had set in and continued till late midnight. We came to know that this singing was associated with the Garbá Dance, a popular folk dance which originated in Gujarát. We learned that the Garbá dance was performed throughout the nine nights of Navarátri and the actual performance began at dusk in some open space in the residential area after the women finished their household work. The name Garbá comes from the Sanskrit word Garbha meaning "womb." The dance celebrates fertility and is performed as a tribute to womanhood and prosperity.

I knew that Navarátri lasted over nine days before the festival of Dussehrá and womenfolk in our region fasted during Navarátri. After the Navarátri, Dussehrá was celebrated by burning effigies of the demon-king Rávana of Sri Lanká as a sign of victory of Lord Ráma over him. Navarátri was the period when young boys from our village played Rám-Lilá in the village centre. But the Navarátri here was completely different, which yielded us to the curiosity of knowing these festivities more closely.

We discovered that the large empty space beyond the quarters for the teaching staff before the quarters for the administrative staff on the east was the venue of garbá dance festivities. The venue was well illuminated with the idol of goddess Ambá standing high in the centre and mainly women folk dressed in special dresses performed the dance in a circular form while going round the idol of the goddess singing and clapping wooden sticks rhythmically. In view of our poor knowledge of the Gujaráti language at that time we did not understand what their singing was about, but the songs were highly melodious. This fascinated some of the students, living in our hostel, from Kerala to join these garbá dances and enjoy the alternative clapping of their sticks with those of other neighbours and their own till late nights. From the many songs sung during these festivities there was one the opening of which I still remember. It sounds as follows: ek banjárin jhoolno jhoolatee hati (a gypsy-woman was swinging on a merry-go-round).

Our academic year lasted up to early march, but we had a short break of some two weeks in between on the occasion of Diwáli. We celebrated Diwáli with our families in Punjáb and passed through the ordeals of two-way travelling by trains smilingly. After the completion of classes we had a couple of weeks for the preparation of written examinations based on syllabuses of subjects taught during the entire year. The final examinations, based on writing answers to sets of questions and on experimental practicals, were conducted by the authorities at the end of march. Thereafter we travelled to Punjáb to have our summer holidays until the beginning of June.

In the first few days in the village I gathered an impression that, even during the vacations, I was financially dependent on my parents and was simply idling away time at home. With these ideas in my mind I went to the District Employment Office, Ferozepur, to get me registered for employment in some school. Soon thereafter I joined Government High School, Sikhwálá, as a science master. Sikhwálá was, and still is, close to Bádal village in Mukatsar Tehsil. I taught science and mathematics to eighth and ninth class students. I had remarkable time teaching there in the cordial atmosphere created by the staff and students. I still remember the taste of food from this village in the form of karhee and tandoori rotis, coupled with a bottle of country-made drink of unknown alcohol content, that I took one evening in the company of a couple of fellow teachers. Some of our students brought this food for us and the fellow teachers acquired the drink from their source. The combination of food and drink were sufficient for me to fall asleep despite my continuous efforts of conversation with the fellow teachers and I entirely forgot to take tea that they prepared after taking the food.

During my brief teaching services in Sikhwálá the results of my examinations had already been declared and the days of my teaching adventures were coming to a fast end. On the last day there, I was indeed moved to see tears flowing from the eyes of some of the students of the eighth class, who somehow became attached to my attitude to them. In any case, I came back to Vidyánagar in Shushil's company soon after my school services to continue studies for the second year.

Some changes had occurred since the previous year. First of all, we were second-year students, and most of our senior MSc colleagues had left Nehru Hall and several new first-year students, admitted for their MSc and MA degrees, had come to stay in it. Among these newcomers were: Tapas Ghosh (Midnapur, West Bengal) for Physics, and Shailendra Singh (Delhi) and Virendra Modi (Sangrur, Punjáb) for Economics. Shailendra Singh was motivated by one of his distant cousins to join this University. This cousin, having the surname Suryawanshi, worked as a Professor of Sociology in the University of Baroda. Virendra Modi was inspired to join this University by his in-laws who had settled in Barodá (Vadodará) after the partition of the country. These in-laws were close relatives of Virendra's family. Therefore, to maintain contact between the two families they married their daughter to Virendra. It turned out that most of these new students stayed in rooms on the first floor of our wing of the hostel. This ensured wonderful communication between us and a lot of fun and jokes out of nothing. Since Bádám and Virendra Modi were somewhat older than us, we began to address them as cháchá and táyá, respectively, and these distinctions they carried with grace. Those were the days when there was green revolution in Punjáb and the MLA from the Abohar area became a cabinet minister in the Congress government.

Soon after the beginning of the academic year some of our senior collegues joined the Department of Physics for PhDs after receiving their MSc degrees. Roop Táku was one of them and was registered under the supervision of Dr Joshi. Like Kotru, Táku began his research work on the study of artificial quartz surfaces, but later he also became interested in the growth of borax crystals from aqueous solutions. He was fascinated by the preponderance of faces on his borax crystals and rich geometrical structures observed on them. Wagh and Bahl were winding up their PhDs. But we kept ourselves engrossed in attending lectures and practical work associated with the programme of our study for the completion of the second year of our MSc. As in the previous year, we travelled to celebrate Diwáli with our families in Punjáb during Diwáli vacations and we had our examinations at the end of March. After the examinations we bade farewell to Vidyánagar to go home and to lead a new life as MSc degree holders, with memories of situations and events of the spent academic year.

Bádám had a talent of narrating real and unreal situations in a humorous and innocent way. He pretended to start a newspaper "Tájá Khabaren" (literally: Fresh News), with news which he himself wrote on a sheet of paper in Urdu and read, with great passion once in two or three weeks, to us. He used Urdu because he studied in Srinagar where he was taught in Urdu. I remember one of his news related to Abohar as follows: "The MLA from Abohar, presently a Minister, was arrested by Police while he was pissing in Street No. 7 of the Old City." He fabricated this news by patching together the information of our MLA becoming a minister from us and the imagination of Street

Number 7 which could be found in different parts, old or new, of practically every city in the country. Once on meeting him I quipped: "You have grown old, Chácha." On hearing this he retorted: "Old you are, old your father is." I understood that he was not in good mood. Therefore, to ease the situation I said: "You are not insulting me, you are insulting your own brother." He did not expect this reply. After a couple of seconds he simply burst into laughter with the words: "Sorry for what I said." And he was the same Bádámcháchá I had known.

For his lectures Professor Patel took assistance of notes, prepared on loosely collected halved A4 sheets, from textbooks listed in our syllabus. We enjoyed repeating his sentence related to probability of occurrence of head and tail of a tossed coin "Fifty percent is the probability for the head up, and fifty percent is the probability for the tail up", using a softened sound of "f" of "fifty" somewhere in between the sounds of "p" and "f." Dr Joshi, as a rule, laughed loudly after reading out his jokes from the margins of the lecture notes he had prepared in his A4 notebook on modern physics. His way of comparison of the disintegration of unstable radioactive particles into stable particles, with the emission of alpha and beta particles and gamma rays, and the indigestion of mortal humans was not so funny for us. Mahendra Agarwál's way of teaching mathematical physics was based on speaking up all that he had stored in his commendable memory.

Colleagues from Kerala were very hard working. Unlike us, they were exceptionally bookish. Among these colleagues, Abraham usually occupied top position in our internal examinations. Bhagwati Agarwál was equally good. Like Mahendra Agarwál, he also hailed from Mount Ábu.

He was in good books of our teachers, because he took his studies here thanks to his acquaintance with Mahendra Agarwál. We noticed that, from time to time, Mahendra Agarwál asked Bhagwati to take care of his house when he was out of station. Mahendra Agarwál lived with his young wife in one of the teachers' apartments in the Colony. I also remember that Maganbhái Patel supervised our practical work. He wanted to visit Delhi for the first time but had problem of accommodation there. My roommate, Sushil, solved this problem. He had some relatives in Delhi and organized Maganbhái's stay with them.

The results of our final examinations were declared when I was in my village. I learned that I secured 595 marks out of 1,000. I could have automatically been grouped into the first division if I had obtained 600 marks. Had I obtained 597 marks, I could have also been grouped into the first division by receiving three so-called grace marks from the University. I consoled myself then by recognizing my poor talent to learn the material from the books and lecture-room notes of the taught syllabus by heart. Sushil fared better than me in this respect. He was indeed a first divisioner. He obtained exactly 600 marks. From the specification of marks in his marksheet of examinations I discerned that he was somewhat rewarded by Maganbhái Patel who conducted our practical examinations. I interpreted this reward as a sign of Maganbhái's gratitude to Sushil for his arrangements of stay in Delhi. Bhagwati was the topper in our group, leaving Abraham in the second position.

During the vacations my family pressed me to get married. It turned out that my father had given a word to the head of a family that his daughter, Pári, and I were a suitable future match. This family was related to us through previous marriages of Pári's two elder sisters with my elder brothers. According to our family it was practically impossible to back out from this marriage because the word of my engagement with Pári was a sacred matter. Disappointed by the results of my MSc degree, I expressed my unwillingness for marriage at that time. I was confident that intellectually I was not worse than most of the first divisioners, including Sushil. Therefore, I had made up my mind to do PhD before my marriage, and explained my position. But all of my arguments fell on a deaf ear in the family. Judging from the prevalent situation, after some time I yielded ultimately to the family dictate and agreed for the arranged marriage with Pári. The marriage was solemnized following family traditions with the meagre resources that the family had at that time.

Among the many relatives and friends, who participated in the solemnization of my marriage ceremony, were the mother and the youngest sister of my school-day friend, Vijay. I remember that the music band that played during the marriage was from our village. It was composed of 4-5 poorly-dressed persons. The engagement of this music band in those days by the family was a reflection of the financial situation of our family and the music group.

Among the different things that served me later after the marriage were the auspicious cash of about two hundred rupees that I received in present as a bridegroom from relatives and friends of our family and a new bicycle received in the dowry. Since I had always been familiar with the financial condition of our family, I made up my mind to take my own decisions regarding my future. My ultimate goal was to undertake PhD studies in Vidyánagar, where

I had known the academic staff reasonably well and had good friends. Therefore, with the amount of money that I had received as a bridegroom, I boarded a train to reach Vidyánagar after two days in early July. There I reached Nehru Hall again. In the Nehru Hall I came to know that Pritpal Tinna (Abohar, Punjáb), Pawan Garg (Barnálá, Punjáb) and Gursharan Cháwlá (Amritsar, Punjáb) had joined the University for their MSc in Physics.

On the following day of my arrival I met Professor Ambubhái Patel in his Office. This Office was located on the ground floor on the northern end of the eastern array of rooms of the Department. I told Professor Patel that I wanted to do my PhD. He agreed to accept me to do my PhD, but told that he did not have the possibility of offering me a scholarship then. He advised me to look about the type of research work being done in the Department. Thus, I became a research student, known as a research scholar in those days. For some days, I stayed in the Nehru Hall with the friends and supported my expenses with the money I had until one day Professor Patel called me to his Office. He communicated to me that I had been awarded a fellowship of University Grants Commission for three years. This fellowship of Rs 250 per month enabled me to complete my PhD thesis.

I was allotted a table to work in the room on the first floor just above Professor Patel's Office. I shared this room with Bhagwati and Damodardás, among others. Bhagwati, who happened to be the topper from our batch, began his research work some days before me and had already been awarded a Gujarát Government fellowship. Damodardás was from the previous-year batch of MSc students. He had been studying the growth of thin films and had his thin-film growth equipment in the central part of the northern array of rooms on the ground floor. Our room in the eastern array, on the first floor, was separated by bath rooms and toilets from the spacious Department Library located at the eastern end of the northern array of rooms. Just below this Library, on the ground floor we did our practical laboratory work in the previous year.

The Department Library had various prescribed journals and selected books on crystal growth relevant to the research work of most of the researchers. In fact, all leading departments had their own libraries, but specialized books and interdisciplinary journals could be borrowed from the main University Library, popularly known as Bháikáká Library.

In the initial period of my research work I concentrated on knowing elements of the field of research of my seniors from their papers published in journals and their PhD theses. The Department Library was a good place for this purpose. There we had access to the journals publishing these papers and to the first-hand information from the authors themselves about their experience as researchers. I discovered that the main research activities of most of them in the Department were concentrated on revealing so-called linear defects, called dislocations, in crystals by dissolving their surfaces in solutions of composition selected by trial and error. This controlled dissolution of crystals was, and still is, known as etching of crystals. The studied crystals were frequently natural minerals procured from the Earth, but artificial crystals grown in the laboratory were also studied. Another type of research activities of a decisive minority was related to the investigation of surfaces of both natural and artificial crystals. Both natural and artificial crystals were usually received from different sources as gifts or purchased from commercial vendors, but after late sixties some researchers began to grow crystals in the Department for their investigations. When I began my research career, the first artificial crystals grown in the Department were of sparingly-soluble inorganic salts. These crystals were obtained by slowly cooling down to room temperature a molten mixture of chemical reactants of the compound of the growing crystals.

A perusal of the PhD theses available in the Department Library indicated that most of their contents on the etching of crystals, studied by their authors, covered a review of the published literature and experimental evidences of reliability of different etching solutions in revealing dislocations in the investigated crystals. Among the frequently cited references in these theses were: a comprehensive book, published in 1950 by Buckley, on crystal growth, a fundamental paper, published in 1951 by Frank, Cabrera and Frank, on the spiral growth theory of crystals in Faraday Transactions, and a paper, published in 1957 by Gilman and his co-workers in Journal of Applied Physics, on the etching of cubic faces of lithium fluoride crystals in water containing different concentrations of ferric ions at room temperature. I went through these references and found the first two positions not of much relevance to the process of etching of crystals. In the Gilman's paper excellent photographic illustrations of change in the shapes of depressions, commonly known as etch pits, formed on lithium fluoride crystals with ferric ion concentrations in water and the possible reason of these changes drew my special attention. However, I was somewhat baffled to note from the theses that different acids and alkalies also produced etch pits of different shapes even on the same face of several other crystals sparingly soluble in water.

About some three months after I began my research work Professor called me to his Office and gave me a large natural galena crystal of cubic shape. When I asked him what to do with this crystal, he simply said: "See what others are doing in the Department." After this I returned to my room. From the book of mineralogy I learned that galena was lead sulphide.

Irrespective of the visitor, Professor Patel always kept the entrance door of his Office open during all of his meetings. This provided an opportunity to persons of good ears, passing by the door, to hear his conversation with the visitor and, to curious-lookers from the side of the western array of rooms, to know who the visitor was. I came to know about this mechanism of functioning of some people in the Department on the day following my meeting with Professor Patel when I met Chandrakánt Desái on my way to my room while climbing stairs above the water cooler. He had recently obtained his PhD degree. He asked me pretentiously: "Why didn't you ask me what you have to do with the crystal?" Irritated by his question I retorted: "You are not my guide. I asked my guide what to do." He felt somewhat uncomfortable with my reply. After an exchange of one more unpleasant sentence between us, we went ahead in opposite directions, with our unaltered positions on the issue.

After having received the galena crystal I began to search the relevant literature of interest for my work on lead sulphide crystals published then from Physics Abstracts segregated in the shelves of the Department Library. I found some papers on stoichiometry in the crystals, dependence of hardness on stoichiometry, formation of punching figures on the cube faces of the crystals, and growth of artificial crystals in silica gels. In two papers I also came across an etching solution to reveal dislocations in these crystals. For preliminary examination of the natural and etched surfaces of my crystal samples I obtained, from the store of the Department, an optical bench microscope, a roll of photographic film and a packet of photographic glass plates.

I installed the bench microscope on my table. The film roll was intended for the photographic work with a camera attached to this microscope. However, the glass plates were to be used in the sophisticated Vickers inverted-type optical microscope, installed long ago, on the ground floor in the room in the vicinity of the water cooler on the east of the southern array of rooms. A part of this room was designed to serve as a dark room for developing photographic films and glass plates. The Vickers microscope was usually used for taking photographs of figures and patterns of layers requiring better optical resolution. The senior colleagues frequently used this microscope to record photographs of so-called multiple-beam interferometric patterns for the estimation of heights of layers and for the analysis of the contour and depth of etch pits on crystal surfaces. Some of them also employed Vickers indenter with this microscope for the determination of hardness of their crystals.

I examined different surfaces of my galena cube that I received from Professor Patel. I found many scratches on them without discernable structures related to growth processes. Then I decided to reveal dislocations on these surfaces by dissolving the crystal cube in a solution of hydrochloric acid containing trace amount of thiourea, according to the recipe published in the literature. On treatment with the solution I found the cube covered with a dark layer. From this dark layer on the cube I reached the conclusion that there could be something wrong with the recipe of the solution. I had known from the published literature that, like our common-salt crystals, galena crystals could be split into smaller parallelopiped-shaped samples with surfaces of the cube. These faces are known as cleavage faces and careful splitting of the crystal, called cleavage, does not introduce new defects in the cleaved samples. Therefore, I decided to obtain small samples from my galena cube for the investigation of dislocations in the crystals. When I examined a couple of these samples after treatment to the known solution of hydrochloric acid containing thiourea for relatively short duration, I observed their surfaces shining and full of tiny etch pits due to dislocations present in the samples. From this observation I concluded that the problem with my galena crystal was due to high density of dislocations estimated by the number of etch pits per unit area. Thus arose the question of exploration of procedures for reduction of the dislocation density in these crystals.

From the published literature I learned that the dislocation density in crystals could be reduced by heating them at a high temperature for some time and then cooling them down slowly to room temperature. This process is known as annealing and is carried out by holding samples in specially-designed ovens, called furnaces, at a temperature somewhat lower than the temperature of their melting in suitable vessels called crucibles. Having this idea in mind and the fact that galena melts at about 1,100 °C, I decided to heat-treat my galena crystal samples at about 800 °C in a platinum crucible kept in an indigenously made furnace.

I chose platinum crucible because of its very high melting temperature. Unfortunately, my experiment proved to be a disaster. I found that my galena crystals melted and the molten mass reacted with the platinum crucible, producing a hole in its bottom. I explained the situation to Professor Patel. He wondered about the outcome of my expensive experiment of losing a platinum crucible, but consoled me for the loss and advised me to repeat the experiment in a crucible of some other material. Following his advice, I chose cheaper silica crucible and repeated my experiment with the annealing. This time the appearance of samples remained unchanged. As expected, I also found a low density of etch pits on their surfaces when I treated them with a mixture of hydrochloric acid and thiourea. This first successful experiment motivated me later to devise more etching solutions for revealing dislocations and to study the effect of dislocation density on the hardness of my galena crystals using a Vickers indenter with the Vickers microscope.

During my annealing experiments I felt that one galena cube was not sufficient for the research work to complete my PhD thesis. In view of this I requested different people to send me natural as well as laboratory-grown crystals. I also planned to grow my own lead sulphide crystals in the laboratory. Since stringent laboratory conditions were required for their growth from the vapour and molten phases, I thought of growing them by a method which demanded less resources. The only choice in this connection was growth in silica gels. Two papers on the growth of lead sulphide crystals had been published at that time.

In response to my requests, I received generous gifts of natural galena crystals from Kinam Sang of Geological

Survey of Korea, Seoul, some natural galena crystals from
Álmora from the Director of Geological Survey of India,
Dehrádun, and a large piece of laboratory-grown crystal
from the melt from R. Thyágarájan of Solid State Physics
Laboratory, New Delhi. I had known from the published
literature that Thyágarájan had worked before in the Institute of Crystallography of the USSR in Moscow, with Aida
A. Urusovkaya, on the deformation of lead sulphide and
cesium iodide crystals, but I did not know him personally.

I remember the name Kinam Sang from his initials
similar to mine. Moreover, examination of the surfaces
of his natural galena crystals showed rich structures of
well-preserved layers forming beautiful elevations due to
growth in the Earth's interior. In order to understand
the mechanism of the formation of these structures I had
to go through the literature published before in this area.
Among this literature, I was especially fascinated by the
photographic illustrations of evidences of growth processes
in the book published in 1953 on spiral growth and dislocations by Ajit Ram Verma and several papers published
mainly during the sixties on the surfaces of various minerals by Ichiro Sunagawa. At that time Verma worked in the
National Physical Laboratory, Delhi, and Sunagawa was
affiliated with the Geological Survey of Japan. Sunagawa
used his original phase contrast microscopy for the examination of mineral surfaces. It was already the second half
of 1969 at that time.

Some colleagues had been exploring the possibility of
using thermal evaporation of their crystals as a reliable
method for revealing dislocations in the form of visible pits
produced on their surfaces by evaporation. This method
had indeed been reported before in the literature. There-

fore, keeping in mind my experience with heating my lead sulphide crystals in the air at elevated temperature, I carried out experiments with the evaporation of my samples at a controlled temperature in the vacuum by holding them in a special equipment. Instead of nice pits on the surfaces of my samples, I observed small lead sulphide crystals of shining surfaces on the evaporating surfaces of the samples and these new small crystals had much lower dislocation density than the evaporating surfaces of the samples.

Apart from the above experiments on evaporation of crystals, I initiated growth of lead sulphide crystals in silica gels in the Department following the procedure reported in 1966 by Blank and Brenner of USA. I prepared a mixture of dilute aqueous sodium metasilicate solution with hydrochloric acid and added thioacetamide to it, and then allowed the solution to become immobile or firm in partly-filled conventional test-tubes at room temperature. Since this immobile mass is gel-like, it is known as silica gel, which is obtained after some days. Then I poured a dilute aqueous solution of lead chloride or lead acetate above the immobile silica gel. After some days I observed many tiny lead sulphide crystals growing in the gel. I also made attempts to grow these crystals by pouring solutions of thioacetamide and lead chloride in two separate open tubes immersed in the volume of silica gel set in large beakers. Again I obtained many small crystals. My attempts to grow large crystals by changing concentrations of poured solutions of the two reactants in these arrangements proved unsuccessful. Simultaneously with my experiments, I encouraged my younger colleagues, H.L. Bhat and Satish Arora, to carry out experiments for the growth of sparingly-soluble sulphates and tungstates using the two arrangements that

I used. Both of these colleagues grew quite large crystals of very low dislocation density. Since these were the first results of growth of these crystals from gels, these colleagues published the results immediately with Professor Patel as the first author. Strangely, although I was the first to introduce the method of crystal growth in gels in the University and in the Country, including the two-tube method, these authors merely acknowledged my assistance in growing large crystals in one of their papers. These two arrangements of growth from gels are now commonly known as single- and double-diffusion methods.

My senior colleagues, Dámodardás, Táku and Sutáriá, were in the final stages of their investigations, and Kuruvilla Cherian had undertaken his research carrier on diamond when the above sulphates and tungstates were grown in gels. We knew that diamond crystals had been studied before in the Department by different researchers, including publication of a couple of methods for preparing replicas of structures on its surfaces for examination by an electron microscope. Shankarbhái Patel for the last several years and Thákorbhai Patel for the last one year had been studying it. Therefore, we were somewhat pessimistic about Kuruvilla Cherian's future concerning new results on diamond. Dámodardás was busy with writing the manuscript of a paper on thin films and Sutáriá had finished experimental investigation of dislocation structure produced by indentation of magnesium oxide crystals. Koshi and Chaudhari had finalized their PhD theses and Ráju had joined the Department as a Post-doctoral Fellow. Kuruvilla was accommodated in our room, but Thákorbhai mainly remained on the ground floor in the room which served as an entrance to the electron microscope room.

Sutáriá was always clad in khádi kurtá-pyjámá, and we could meet Chaudhari frequently chewing his betels that he had brought with him from the betel-shop in the small market on his way back to the Department after taking morning meals in one of the private messes there nearby. From Kuruvilla Cherian I learned to take black tea in our room. It was the time when the Malyálam movie "Chemeen" was released. A song sung by Manna Dey in this movie was very popular with the colleagues from Kerala. I liked this song which had its beginning something like this: "Mánas mayne varu, madhuram nulli taru ..." I learned the first lines of this song by heart and practised to sing it with the Malyálam accent approved by Kuruvilla. Apart from different songs in Hindi, this Malyálam song was the only one that I learned attentively in my lifetime. My effort of singing this song was indeed rewarded when a fellow research student from Kerala, working in the neighbouring room, entered our room to know who the singer was. He was surprised to see me singing in Malyálam.

All research students had one common trait of research work. They came to the Department at 8 AM, left for morning meals at about 10 AM, and after the meals returned to work in the Department till 6 PM. After taking evening meals many of them also came to work and worked for hours until they finished their planned work. Night hours were found suitable for hardness measurements on samples and multiple-beam interferometry of surfaces. Negligible transport on the surrounding roads during these hours ensured minimal vibrations in the Earth's surface to obtain better reproducibility in hardness measurements and better resolution in interferometric patterns. Most of us worked in this way practically on all days except Sundays.

Some of us had a tea break at about 2 PM when we exchanged our views on all types of matters related and unrelated to us. The place of sipping this afternoon tea was Bháiji's Lorry located at the southern end of the sparsely used dusty street, with patches of wild grass, between the outer western wall of the Girls' Hostel and the eastern wall of the Humanities Building of the University. The Lorry was practically attached to the wall of the Girls' Hostel and, to its west, it faced windows of rooms and lecture halls of the Humanities Building. The windows could be opened inside but were usually kept shut, which left enormous empty space outside in the wall. In the empty space of one of these windows we kept sheets of local newspapers, on which we used to sit after spreading on the grassy ground in the street while taking tea and gossiping on topics of the day. Many research scholars from other Departments also frequently joined us during these tea-breaks. Among these were: Shailendra Singh and Ávaddán Cháran from the Department of Economics, and I.L. Kothári from the Department of Biology. Cháran's research was related to agricultural economics under the supervision of Professor V.S. Vyás, but Shailendra Singh's commerce-related work was under the supervision of Dr Adhivaryu. Professor Vyás was the Head of the Department of Economics and Dr Ad-hivaryu was a reader there. Kothári worked with Professor J.J. Shah, who was also the Head of the Department of Botany. However, because of my closeness to Cháran and Singh, I knew personally the entire academic staff of the Department of Economics. Apart from Prof. Vyás and Dr Adhivaryu, there were two lecturers: Srivástava and

Bágchi. I had frequent contacts with the latter two. Later Arunbhái Patel joined them as a lecturer.

Srivástava came from Uttar Pradesh and Bágchi hailed from Bengál. Whenever we met, both of them were dressed like us and spoke in Hindi with their distinct accent. Both Srivástava and Bágchi lived in service apartments in the University Colony. Srivástava lived alone as a bachelor, but I did not find anything unusual in his way of life. Bágchi lived with his spouse and two small kids. The family spoke in Bengáli at home and cultivated Banglá traditions. Arunbhái Patel came from some nearby village. He was a follower of Swaminárávan variant of Hinduism, which is prevalent in Gujarát, and always carried a red-coloured mark on his forehead as a sign of religious affiliation. Arunbhái was not the only disciple of the Swaminárávan faith. We could equally see many more in the University, especially in the Department of Chemistry and the University Administration, belonging to this faith. Pilgrimages to the huge complex of Swaminárávan Temple in Vadtál by the disciples were common in those days.

Department of Economics had the Editorial Office of an international journal "Arath Vikás" (Economic Development) published quarterly in English. This journal earned hard currency for the University by publishing research articles of authors from foreign countries.

We enjoined giving nicknames to our teachers and frequently addressed each other as well by nicknames. These nicknames were used in the discussions during our tea-breaks. One of these discussions was on an imaginary topic related to our research supervisor, Professor Patel, whom we called "Káká." The topic was: "Why is Káká's undershirt dirty?." Arguments advanced in the discussion were that Káki (i.e. Professor's wife) was busy in the leadership of the women in the Colony, his son was busy in minting money, his elder daughter was on honeymoon, and his younger daughter was busy in the search of a suitable husband. Since all knew that our supervisor's wife was immensely involved in social activities, his elder daughter got married some time before and the younger one was a student in one of the local colleges, these explanations appeared not only logical but offered us long amusement.

Most of us liked to rest on Sundays. Some of us living in the Nehru Hall preferred to watch some good movie in the afternoon in one of the three movie halls in the neighbouring Ánand. To watch a movie we travelled in a group to Ánand by the local bus. There was no big problem in purchasing entrance tickets to watch a movie. I personally knew the managers of two of these movie halls, and when tickets for a show were sold out before our arrival, the managers made arrangements to accommodate us on additional chairs in the stairs of the halls. After the movie we went to some restaurant to have some food and tea. Exception to the above routine was to watch some movie in the evening on other days. On such occasions we used our own bicycles or bicycles hired from the bicycle store run in the small market on our way to the Department. When there was no good movie shown in the cinema halls or we did not want to work in the Department, some of us preferred to spend afternoons in listening to songs from the latest films in the only bar in the small market or to visit a small Gurudwárá close to the Railway Station in Ánand. This Gurudwárá was situated in a narrow street in the neighbourhood of Santokh Mathároo's house. He lived with his parents and a younger brother. Prakásh Sálvi also lived with his mother in a house nearby. After worshiping in the Gurudwárá, we usually visited the house of one of these friends, where their mothers served us some snacks and tea devotedly.

Those were the days of films like Árádhaná, Prem Pujári and Gambler, with Kishore Kumár being the top male singer. I liked his style of singing songs with initial humming and yodelling. Among his different songs I enjoyed singing the song from the film Árádhaná: "Mere sapanon ki ráni kab áyegi tu, áee rut mastáni kab áegi tu?" (The queen of my dreams, when will you come; the crazy season, when will you come?). I frequently sang this song in full voice while going to take tea at Bháiji's Lorry and developing films and photographic plates of photographs of surfaces of crystals, in a specially prepared solution kept in a tray, in the darkroom. I adjusted the time of holding plates and film-rolls in the developing solution in accordance with the verses of these songs. Songs from the latest movies could be heard from radio-sets in the market and from small portable radios hanging on the shoulders of local milk vendors, riding their bicycles, from the neighbouring villages. On our way to the Department, crowds of students from the nearby colleges and other young bystanders, living in nearby hostels and houses, could be seen standing before the betel-selling shop in the small market every Wednesday evening to know the ranking of the latest popular film songs played in Binaca Geetmálá on Radio Ceylon by Amin Sáyáni. These crowds were measures of craze of listening to the film music in those days.

I had developed a habit of singing some song whenever I entered Nehru Hall in the evening after finishing my work of the day in the Department. Once the hostel superintendent saw me singing in this way. He simply smiled, but politely advised me not to do so in the future.

Atmosphere in the Nehru Hall was wonderful during the days of my research work. We liked to exchange a couple of words with all we met in the corridor. We also enjoyed meeting each other in their rooms and made jokes of all sorts. When Tapas Ghosh was in the second year of his MSc, being senior to them, he had become very close to Pritpal Tinna, Pawan Garg and Gursharan Cháwlá. In his characteristic Banglá-style Hindi, Ghosh usually teased Cháwlá by calling him mini-Sardár because of his stature. I frequently saw Cháwlá, in his room with his colleagues from Kerala, discussing topics taught in the lectures and derivation of some equations there, in Hindi as the common language of communication. Sometimes he became so engaged in these discussions that he even forgot to use the right Hindi word or verb and used Punjábi equivalent. Once I noted that he used the Punjábi verb "labhaná" for "dhoondhaná (find)", but his colleague from Kerala simply nodded as if he understood everything. Cháwlá was very religious and said his prayers daily from the holy Gutaká. Garg and Tinná were different, but they were always affable to others. Once Mahendra Agarwál told Pawan Garg to see him at home. To this Garg replied innocently: "OK Sir, I will see you." We were somewhat amused to hear the way he said: "I will see you."

It was the era of Illustrated Weekly of India, with Khushwant Singh as its Editor. Occasionally, its weekly editions contained large colour photographs of prominent Hollywood and Bollywood actresses printed on combined even-odd pages in its middle. We cultivated a tradition to pick some of these photographs from these editions and decorate the dull white walls and ceiling of our room by them. Once during an inspection, the hostel superintendent noticed the decoration in our room. He informed us that he disliked this and advised us to remove the photographs from the room. I indeed removed some of them. Tarun Kumár Dás was my roommate at that time.

It was the beginning of the second year of my research work. It was morning and I was in my room in the hostel when someone knocked at its entrance door. On opening the door I saw a tall young man standing before me with rolled bedding and a bag. He told me that Tapas Ghosh had directed him to meet me and gave me a letter from Ghosh. Shyly he spoke in poor Banglá-style Hindi. I requested him to take rest in my room and to tell me when he arrived from Midnápur. Ramesh Setiá from our city, Abohar, had also arrived then for his MSc in Biology. I did not know him before, but I had known that his father owned a cycle store in the city.

Dás told me that he had been admitted for his MSc in the Department of Chemistry. Later I introduced Dás to other companions in the hostel and discussed about our possible roommates. Since Dás and Setiá were new in our company, we reached the consensus that the best option for us would be to accommodate Dás with me and Setiá with Cháwlá. Dás accepted the proposal gladly. When I informed him about my inability to buy milk everyday early in the morning for our daily tea, he agreed immediately to buy milk and prepare tea for both of us everyday morning. He indeed kept his promise. We lived together on the first floor in the first room on the left of the corridor in the eastern wing of the hostel for two years without a single word of discord and mutual disrespect.

Research students like me belonging to our Department, living in the Nehru Hall, relished their meals together as a group in the mess where we shared the same table and talked on different matters. Occasionally, colleagues from other departments also accompanied us during these meals. Sundays offered these colleagues this possibility, and the days of feasts were especially lively in this connection. We never cared to criticize the mess contractor for some food dish that fell short of our expectation regarding its quality and savour. When this contractor was not present to hear our complaint in the mess during the hours of a meal, we left a message of our displeasure with the man at the counter, called Mehtá, and invited the contractor to meet us as early as possible in the mess to address our grievance.

During the tenure of one of the contractors we observed that, instead of pure wheat flour used for baking loaves to be served in the mess, the baked loaves served to us contained sufficient amount of much cheaper bájari flour. We drew the attention of the contractor, but he did not heed to our complaint for a good couple of months. Irritated by his behaviour some of us also did not pay for the monthly meals for the last months.

During one of our morning meals, when the contractor was sitting at the counter, we loudly began to talk about our expectation of good meals and delicious feasts. During this discussion someone among us said that we would arrange a feast for the contractor if he was unwilling to do so in the mess for us. The contractor felt offended from our discussion and the mess dues to him. Immediately thereafter, the contractor complained to Professor Patel,

Research Guide of many of us, that we did not want to pay his mess dues. Professor Patel was the Warden of our hostel at that time.

Some days after the above incidence of our discussion of meals and feasts, Professor Patel called our group of 7-8 participants in the mess to his Office. We entered his Office and stood in a row close to the door timidly as if we were his most obedient students. He stared at us and then simply instructed us to pay the mess dues. We argued that we were unwilling to do so because of the quality of meals he had served. The Professor did not expect this from our group. He frowned on us and said: "Get out of here." Immediately on hearing this we left Professor's Office with bowed heads and reached our working tables on the first floor. After this visit to Professor's Office we began to have our meals in a private mess situated on our way to the Department. A couple of months later the contractor also resigned from running the hostel mess.

The Department Library not only enabled us to follow the published literature from the journals and books it had, but also served us in different ways because of its large space. Prakásh Sálvi, who looked after the in-coming and out-going correspondence in the Department and was responsible for typing it on a type-writer, typed rough drafts of PhD theses during the Office hours, which research students subsequently gave to their research supervisors for their comments and corrections. After receiving back the drafts from them, the research students introduced appropriate modifications in the drafts and Prakásh typed the final versions of PhD theses after the Office hours. Because typing of theses of research students was not a part of his service responsibility, the writers paid for this work.

Like other officials in the small Department Secretariat, Prakásh was always highly cooperative and friendly. For this reason I fondly called him Pyárelál.

The Library was equally ideally suited to discuss current results and research problems of our mutual interest, and to introduce manually corrections in each of the five typed copies of final theses. Moreover, it had excellent temperature to take rest, and even naps, on the easychairs during the long hours of summer noons. In view of the large space one senior colleague also used it, as a free lodge, for some time instead of paying for accommodation in the hostel. He justified this decision on the ground that he could not complete his PhD thesis during the scholarship period. During the days of his lodging in the Library he merely went out to take his morning and evening meals and to buy some petty articles.

The teaching staff usually worked between 10 AM and 5 PM. Exception to this routine was Professor Patel, who sometimes came to the Department at 8 AM and left it somewhat before 10 AM for his morning meals. After the meals he returned to the Department where he stayed till evening. He always sent one of the peons every 10-15 days for each of his research students to inform him of the progress of their research work. It was indeed a mental exercise for most of us to explain the progress in such a short period. However, with the passage of time I reached the conclusion that one should always keep some of the results undisclosed for lean days of progress. This practice indeed worked well later.

When Professor Patel was in the Department and did not have his lectures, he usually remained in his Office studying something or correcting manuscript of some research paper of his students, enquiring about the progress of their research, advising administrative and teaching staff, and having meetings with visitors. When he was present in his Office, we could occasionally see some of the staff members walking on the opposite side of the Professor's Office with photographic plates held at a distance in their right hands and pretending as if they were examining them. Since practically all of these staff members had completed their PhDs with the Professor, we interpreted their conduct as a method of impressing upon the latter their great involvement in research. This behaviour of the staff members during the working hours was indeed an indicator of Professor Patel's presence in the Department.

The entire teaching staff, including Professor Patel, travelled to the Department by riding their bicycles parked in the cycle-stand behind the main entrance, and the teaching staff always left the Department after the Professor had already left it. Before his departure, one of the peons picked Professor's bicycle out of the cycle-stand and waited for him to ride home. Once Professor Patel left the Department somewhat earlier. As soon as he left, most of the staff members picked out their bicycles to ride home, but they saw the Professor returning to the Department. Hurriedly, the poor fellows parked their bicycles back in the bicycle-stand and returned to their rooms. It so happened that the Professor returned because the hind wheel of his bicycle needed pumping. It was a great fun for us to see all this happening before us.

It was a common knowledge that Professor Patel followed the same route of his bicycle ride to and from the Department. Some senior colleagues used this knowledge by following a different route to come to the Department not at 8 AM, but after morning meals, when Professor Patel traditionally returned from there before 10 AM to have his meals. On his way to the Department our senior colleague, Ráju, indeed preferred to enjoy this method of avoiding an encounter with the Professor.

In the initial period of my research work I did not have a bicycle to reach the Department from our hostel. In those days I rarely walked to and from the Department alone. Our walks in a group to the Department were relatively smooth because of constraint of reaching there at a specified time, but my companions shunned to return to our hostel with me on foot in the evening. The reason was that I had cultivated a habit of exchanging a couple of sentences of goodwill with most of acquaintances I met on our way. Since I considered it impolite to do so while walking, I always stopped for some moments. This earned me the recognition of "Passenger train" from my companions, and I had to be highly cautious that they did not suffer excessively in my company and penalise me by leaving me behind to follow them alone.

When we were doing our MSc, we met Vinoobhái Patel who was doing his MA in English. After his studies he taught English in Nalini and Arvind Arts College and later joined H.M. Institute of English. Both of these institutions were in the University Campus and were not far from our Department. Because of the proximity of our institutions, we frequently met each other either taking tea at Bháiji Lorry or walking somewhere in the small market. And with time we became great friends.

A large number of students in the local colleges in the University Campus were from the villages of old Kherá district. This trend, combined with the general policy of recruitment of teachers for these colleagues from qualified candidates from the area, created opportunities that these teachers not only knew their students, but had family relations. The college teachers also knew many of our local colleagues, and Vinoobhái was not an exception. He hailed from Vaherá village in old Petlád táluká, not far away from Vidyánagar to its south. His family owned agricultural fields.

We came to know that the Patels of Kherá district married in their own circles of villages and did not approve of marriages outside their own circles. If someone went against this tradition, the bridegroom and the bride were considered outcasts. It so happened that a young Patel boy, Rajanikánt, of one circle of villages fell in love with a Patel girl, Praveená, of another circle of villages. Both of them were students in a college in Vidyánagar. The families of the boy and the girl were against their matrimony. When attempts by the two families failed to dissuade the young couple from marriage and the latter decided to marry without blessings of their families, our Vinoobhái came to their rescue. He knew them not only as students but also knew their situation.

The young couple first rented a room to live on Bákrol Road, not far away from our Department. Thanks to Vinoobhái, Roop Táku and I, among others, also became friends of the young couple. We began to visit them whenever someone of us found some time to spend with them. Our main role of these visits was to allay their impression that they were alone in this World. During summer vacations a theft took place in the house when Rajanikánt and Praveenában were in Ahmedábád. The responsibility of informing them of the theft fell on me. In connection with this theft, I also visited the Police Station in Ánand. Unfortunately, the thieves were never caught.

After sometime Rajanikánt and Praveenáben rented another accommodation in one of the houses, with jasmine flowers in its surrounding, not far off from our hostel, Nehru Hall, on our way to the Department. In long summer days whenever I visited them, Praveenáben frequently instructed me fondly to straighten my "spine" on the bed in the room. Later when their daughter Sejal was born, we began to try different skills to stop her weep. I remember a song that I got to sing her in those days: "Sejal re tu mat roná ... (O Sejal, do not weep ...)."

The above example of unapproved marriage by families of bridegroom and bride is not isolated. One of the students of the Department of Biology, who lived in our hostel, also decided to marry a girl he loved. However, he did not have the right pair of pants for this occasion. I knew this boy well. He asked me whether I could help him by lending him one of my pairs of pants. I showed him my different pairs of pants, and he chose one of them, of light green colour, to borrow on the occasion of marriage. Some days later he got married. After the marriage this gentleman entirely forgot to return the pair of pants. I also considered it unwise to ask him to return it.

I was always interested in knowing the culture of crops in this part of Gujarát because of my agricultural background. One day I asked Vinoobhái to do me the favour of showing his family fields and crops they cultivated. He agreed and specified the day of our visit to his village Vaherá.

Accompanied by Vinoobhái, our group of five or six colleagues travelled on the planned day to Vaherá village by state transport bus service and alighted at its bus-stand close to the Cooperative Society Building and its spacious ground on the outskirts of the village. Then we walked to Vinoobhái's house situated in its central part. There he introduced us to his father, Motikáká, elder brother, Natubhái and other members of the family. There he also introduced us to his wife that he married again recently. I compared the members of Vinoobhái's family with mine and imagined that Motikáká was somewhat younger than my father and Natubhái was older than us by about seven or eight years. I found that Motikáká preferred to smoke his own tobacco in his freshly-lit hooká instead of beedees widely used for smoking in Gujarát. I saw tobacco leaves drying in the compound of their house. From the way of behaviour of Motikáká and his eldest son, Natubhái, I understood that Motikáká had entrusted the responsibility of household matters to this son. During our stay there I noted that it was Natubhái who looked after us. He also took us to their wide fields where they grew tobacco plants. At that time I thought that crops of tobacco plants, like Natubhái's, were pillars of tobacco industry in that part of India.

All festivals are jovial but the festival of Holi in Gujarát is special. Apart from painting colourful powders on the faces of young males and females known to us, we enjoyed visiting, one after another, houses of our colleagues and teachers living in University quarters, exchanging greetings and sharing different freshly-cooked snacks served there. Once in 1970, students and teachers of our Department also celebrated Holi by eating and singing together one evening in its central grassy compound. On that occasion some of the research students (Roop Táku, Satish Arorá, H.L. Bhat and me, among others) had a performance of singing a song. Táku and I wrote the text and Bhat composed music for it on a harmonium. The first line of the text was as follows: "Sáthio, áo milake Holi khelen re... (Colleagues, let us play Holi together)."

When my attempts to grow only a few large lead sulphide crystals from silica crystals using different arrangements turned out be futile, I decided to examine their surfaces using the bench microscope standing on my table. I also examined natural surfaces of galena minerals that I had obtained as gifts and structures on cleaved surfaces of annealed crystals. Apart from these investigations, I carried out hardness measurements under different experimental conditions and devised various solutions for revealing dislocations on the cube faces of the heat-treated crystals. At the same time I began to systematize these results in the form of chapters of my future PhD thesis.

I systematized the results of surface structures on the crystals grown in silica gels. These results were the first on crystals grown in gels. Since I did not have much experience with surface structures, I sent these results to Dr Sunagawa, of Geological Survey of Japan, for his comments. A couple of months later, I received his comments which were very encouraging. I also wrote my first manuscript based the results of my experiments on the growth of small crystals by heating samples in vacuum for publication. This manuscript was published in 1971 in Journal of Crystal Growth, which was established three years ago.

Based on my results I prepared drafts of a couple of more manuscripts for publication in journals, requested Prakásh Sálvi to type them, and then gave the typed drafts to Professor Patel for his comments and corrections.

I also made efforts to discuss the contents of one of these manuscripts with him but he remained unmoved. I understood that he was not much convinced by their contents.

Senior research colleagues occasionally spoke jokingly about corrections made in the contents of drafts of original manuscripts by the supervisors. They advised us to keep uncorrected drafts in our table-drawers because contents of corrected drafts after another correction by the supervisors were likely to return to the contents of their first drafts.

In the last months of 1990, Sutáriá was finalizing his thesis. He had amassed a lot of experimental results on magnesium oxide crystals which he had obtained from some commercial source. He had written a rough draft of his thesis, but he had problems with the English grammar. He requested us to check the contents of the draft. I offered him my services. I was highly impressed by his grasp of the issues described in the draft. When I asked what he wanted to write, he explained in Hindi vividly what he meant. His only difficulty was to express his ideas in English. With his assistance and perpetual explanation, we finalized the draft of his thesis, which Prakásh Sálvi began to type on his type-writer somewhere in the beginning of 1971. Sutáriá's thesis also aroused my interest in carrying out more experimental work on our understanding of process of etching of sparingly-soluble dielectric crystals some years later.

After the finalization of Sutáriá's thesis, I began to prepare a rough draft of my thesis and requested Prakásh Sálvi to type its chapters successively. When the typed version of the rough draft was ready, I informed Professor Patel that I had written the draft of my thesis and asked him what to do with it. He called Dr Mahendra Agarwál and asked him, in my presence, to check my thesis. Immediately thereafter, I passed on the typed rough draft to Dr Agarwál. And it was the beginning of summer vacations.

After the vacations Professor Patel called me to his Office and informed that the manuscript was badly written. When I enquired more about the main problems, he told me to contact Dr Agarwál. I contacted Dr Agarwál immediately, who told me that the results of structures on cleaved surfaces were not good and the draft was written in poor English. I had indeed worked hard in writing the results on cleavage faces and knew the language reasonably well. Therefore, his remarks somewhat surprised me, but I swallowed them without a word of discord. I informed him that I could omit the part of the thesis dealing with cleavage faces and request one of the lecturers of English to check its language. When he enquired about this person, I told that it was Shabir Ahmed. He was somewhat surprised to know that I knew him, but he agreed with my concept.

Shabir Ahmed lived in an apartment close to Agarwál's apartment in the University Colony. Shabir Ahmed hailed from Delhi and I had known him well. He was a lecturer in the Institute of English, where our friend, Vinoobhái Patel, also taught English.

I contacted Shabir and narrated the situation. He told that his wife had gone to visit her brother in Bhopál and would stay there some more days. Therefore, we could take up the correction work in the draft in his apartment immediately. It took us some two weeks to check my draft. At the end, he summed up the work of checking the draft by saying that even some of the lecturers of his Institute could not write better than what I had written. I felt greatly flattered by his words and thanked him for his correction work.

I took the corrected draft of the thesis to Prakásh Sálvi and requested him to type the text of pages that were modified significantly. This was the period when Bhagwati Agarwál began to finalize the draft of his thesis. He asked for my assistance in this work. I agreed and undertook the task of checking his version of the draft. Additionally, I kept an eye on the progress of retyping of corrections by Prakásh in the draft of my thesis. Finally, following the suggestion of Professor Patel to pass on the final draft of the thesis for the approval of Dr Mahendra Agarwál, I handed over the final version to the latter as soon as Prakásh retyped the appropriate pages.

A couple of weeks later, Dr Agarwál informed me that the draft was acceptable. Then I began to prepare copies of photographs of figures for inclusion in the final version of the thesis. After the completion of this work of preparation of photographs in the dark room, I approached Prakásh again to plan his schedule of typing the final version of my thesis after his Office hours. This work also took another couple of weeks. Then some of the colleagues and I segregated the typed version of the thesis into its original and four copies, enumerated from first to fourth, and at appropriate places inserted additional pages of pasted photographs of figures numbered consecutively. We finished this work of preparation of the thesis by verifying the typed text and pasted photographs in each of its copies. Finally, I gave these segregated copies for binding in Ánand. I collected them back from the binder after some days. It was the end of October.

The Department Library was again found to be the right place to carry out the entire work of typing and segregation of copies of the thesis and verification of their final contents. Similarly, the binder in Ánand provided excellent services. In fact, the above observations corroborated the experience of our predecessors.

In the beginning of November I submitted three copies, original and first and second copies, to the University for evaluation for the award of a PhD degree to me. Then I began to wind up my stay in Vidyánagar and made plans of travel to my village. I could made reservation for my journey by railways in the first days of December. When I travelled in December, the trains faced black out during night due to war of freedom of Bangládesh. However, I reached home safely without any untoward incident during the journey. At home, I began to assist one of my elder brothers in our family farming.

Somewhere in March 1972, I received a letter from the University Office informing me that, in view of favourable reports on my PhD thesis from its referees, I was expected to have a viva voce examination for the award of a PhD degree to me in the middle of April. I remember that one of the reviewers was Professor N.S. Pándyá of M.S. University of Baroda. I reached Vidyánagar and contacted Professor Patel. He showed me the reports, which I found praising my work. Professor informed me that my examination would be held in Baroda in Professor Pándyá's Office.

On the day of my viva voce examination I reached Barodá. There Professor Pándyá, as one of the referees, and Professor Patel, as my research supervisor, were present in Professor Pándyá's Office. Everything went smoothly in the examination and both of the examiners congratulated me for the successful examination. Some days later, I obtained personally an official document of the award of a PhD degree to me from the University Office.

After the publication of my only research paper in 1971, I could publish, in later years, seven more research papers based on the results of my PhD thesis, and some of them indeed earned me later good recognition in the scientific community. The above period of research activities relieved me from my antitalent of learning different things by heart.

October 2022

3

DAYS IN SOCIALISM

IN THE HEYDAYS OF SOCIALISM the Soviet Union made enormous efforts to propagate its achievements in different walks of the life of its citizens by distributing across the Globe profoundly illustrated magazines published on glittering white paper in various vernaculars. One could easily buy these magazines in newspaper kiosks of small towns and big cities at throw-away prices. In those days I was more interested in completing my higher education than buying and reading these magazines. In fact, I was content then with my familiarity of the life of the people of this region of the World from my college days when I read the English translation of the Russian writer Lev Tolstoy's short story "God sees the truth but waits" in the compilation of selected literature in the subject of English.

Some time later the results of my master's studies were a big disappointment for me. I missed first division by a couple of marks, although, judging from the results of my colleagues, I thought I deserved it. Filled with anger at this failure, I made up my mind to undertake doctoral studies and prove my worth. Thus, I became a researcher in the field of Solid State Physics at Sardar Patel University in the beginning of July of 1968, and began to dig into the published literature in the field of my future research work.

During my doctoral studies I found in our Department Library journals like Soviet Physics – Solid State and Soviet Physics – Crystallography, translated into English in the USA by Consultant Bureau from the Russian originals.

I was immensely impressed by the contents of some of the papers in the field of dissolution and deformation of crystals published in these journals by authors affiliated to the Institute of Crystallography in Moscow. This time was somewhat more than a decade after the spiral growth theory of crystals was proposed, roughly a decade after the first observations of movement of dislocations in crystals were made, three years after the publication of a book on crystallization in gels, and a specialized journal devoted to growth of crystals was founded. Those were the days of hectic scientific activities all over the World, which enticed me to know more and more of advances in different research areas from the stream of issues of journals freshly arriving regularly in the Department Library and to carry out experimental research work based on novel concepts, instead of making similar measurements on different crystals, as was the routine in those days. I was satisfied with the growth of my lead sulphide crystals from silica gels, a method that I introduced first in the country, but, despite my unsuccessful attempts to grow them to sufficiently large dimensions, the method became very popular in subsequent years for the growth of a variety of crystals in different laboratories across the country. Experimental work on localized deformation of my crystals by punching their surfaces and on various solution compositions to reveal dislocations on them also gave me great satisfaction.

After three years of experimental work I compiled my results in the form of dissertation which, after corrections and modifications, I submitted for the award of my PhD degree in the beginning of December. Those were the last days of liberation of Bangládesh from the yoke of West Pákistáni rulers and there was a complete blackout at night

in the trains. I experienced this when I travelled by train
from Vadodara to my native village in Punjáb. A couple of
days later the Pákistán Army surrendered and Bangládesh
was born with Shaikh Mujibur Rahman as its undisputed
leader.

Some months later when reviewers' reports on my dissertation reached the University, a viva voce examination
was arranged. Based on the outcome of this examination
and the reviewers' reports, the University awarded me a
PhD degree in July. This PhD degree proved helpful to me
to get the job of an assistant professor in the only college
in Sangaria, a city some thirty kilometres from my native
village. Unfortunately, this job was temporary and my
credentials for the post that I occupied here proved insufficient after this duration. The selection committee chose
a non-PhD fresher known to the son of the President's
daughter of the managing committee of the college. Then
I decided to embrace a farmer's garb and assist my elder
brother in modernization of our family agricultural fields.

With my brother I harvested in the fields practically
two successive crops. However, the initial zeal of adventur-
ous work with the crops in the family fields slowly faded
away and I began to feel that my disposition did not suit
this profession. During this later period, this feeling of un-
suitability motivated me to prepare from my unpublished
dissertation some manuscripts for publication in different
journals and to apply for post-doctoral fellowships.

There was a dearth of many things in those days for the
farmers. Water in our canal for the irrigation of the fields
was frequently siphoned out on its way by wide rubber
pipes laid on the canal bank, availability of fertilizers in the
market mainly rested on the whims of depot holders respon-

sible for their sale, and sugar was distributed occasionally in the village on ration cards by an authorized agent of dubious selection by the administrative authorities. Rumours were rampant that the local MLA had no scarcity of water to irrigate his fields and truck-loads of fertilizers were being diverted to his house. The greatest dismay was that on one occasion during the spreading of phosphate fertilizer in the fields I discovered dry horse-dung combined with it in two bags purchased before with enormous patience.

The outcome of all the three applications that I sent was very consolatory. I was directed to work in my Alma Mater as a Pool Officer. It was an interim position financed by Council of Scientific and Industrial Research to find a stable job in near future. I complied with this immediately. A professor from Rensselaer Polytechnic wrote to wait for about six months until his research grant was approved. In the third case, there was an invitation to appear before a committee in New Delhi for an interview for a post-doctoral fellowship in USSR. I remember that, during the interview by a selection committee of about a dozen members, I was asked to explain why I did not use an electron microscope instead of an optical microscope that I used to examine my crystal samples for my PhD thesis and whether I had been in the USSR before. My responses to these questions were simple. I told that all information that I wanted to have from the examination of my samples I could obtain by using an optical microscope and that I had never visited the USSR before but I knew of good work being done in the Institute of Crystallography in Moscow and I intended to work there. The outcome of this interview was that I was selected for a two-year fellowship. Official letter in this connection contained the information that in the beginning of November I was expected to reach Moscow first and then to Tashkent State University.

The choice between fellowships in USA and USSR remained a dilemma for some time, but after judging different pros and cons I decided to accept fellowship from the USSR. Curiosity of knowing the other side of the existing tall curtain, inclination of seeing social justice in everyday life and confidence in visiting USA someday in my later life went in favour of this decision. Thus, with the help of a travel agent I got my passport from Regional Passport Office, Ahmedábád, received a visa, purchased a ticket financed partially by my friends, and landed one afternoon at Seremetova Airport in Moscow with 20 USD in my pocket. I exchanged this amount of currency at Pálam Airport in Delhi at the official rate of about Rs 7.5 per USD and the amount of 20 USD was entered in my passport. Those were the days when more money exchange was forbidden for travellers abroad.

At the exit gate of the Seremetova Airport I could see a tall young blond waving a banner briskly to receive travellers like me. When I produced my official letter to him, he directed me to an empty bus, fabulously lit inside, standing close by. Some minutes later two Nepálese boys boarded the bus, and the bus left the airport with three passengers accompanied by the blond guide. After travelling for some half an hour, we arrived at a hotel in the city. Our young guide took us to the reception desk of the hotel, where we were allotted accommodations and given coupons for three-time meals during our stay from the hotel restaurant on the ground floor. Here at this desk I came to know that my Nepálese co-passengers had come to study for their undergraduate degree. Later our guide took us to a nearby supermarket to equip us with winter clothes and shoes for our survival in the severe winters awaiting us here during our stays.

Next day I visited the Indian Embassy and changed with one of the Embassy Officials attending me my twenty dollars into roubles for some urgent needs. I learned that I changed the money at the official exchange rate. It was indeed a great excitement to travel by metro train for the first time. In the evening of the third day of my arrival, my guide took me to a railway station to get into an express train to Tashkent and introduced me to the female attendant of a sleeping car of the train and handed over my ticket to her. This lady allotted me a berth in the company of three other passengers, a Russian travelling to Ekaterinburg and an Uzbek couple travelling to Tashkent. Communication between us remained a challenging task during this journey because these co-passengers mainly spoke among themselves in Russian but my knowledge of this language was confined entirely to reading translations of scientific literature published in English from it. When my efforts to find any sign of similarity between the languages they spoke and I knew proved unsuccessful, we tried all our skills to communicate in English. Their narration of Nehru's political stature and Ráj Kapoor's films, including a reference to red Russian cap in one of the songs of the film "Mr 420" did bring me closer to them, but difficulty in communication was certainly a persistent barrier in this closeness. In response to their question of our family occupation in one of the conversations during the journey when I told that we were farmers, they certainly took me for a bourgeoisie. They were indeed great hosts in the train restaurant where I could neither decipher the menu nor order the dishes I wanted to eat. On the third day we reached Tashkent. When we alighted the train at the Tashkent Railway Station, sensing my problems of language and travelling in a completely unknown city, the Uzbek couple was generous enough to hire a taxi at the taxi stand outside and take me to the Administrative Office of the University. The Foreign Affairs Section thereafter took care of my academic stay there and I was accommodated in a students' hostel nearby.

The first thing that the Foreign Affairs Section did was organization of teaching of Russian language and an experienced teacher, Svetlana Majidovna, was entrusted this job to teach our small group of some Egyptian students accompanied by me. These Egyptians had come here for their Candidate of Sciences degrees, equivalent to PhDs according to the British system. Svetlana's intensive efforts enabled us to speak some simple sentences within a month. But I began to speak better than my Egyptian colleagues. The reason was that they talked among themselves in Arabic, but I had more practice to converse with others in Russian. This initial period of my stay immediately after my arrival there in Tashkent indeed proved a boon to learn Russian language speedily because then I knew neither compatriots to talk in Indian languages nor other foreigners to talk in English. Some time later a young teacher, Aziza Alimovna, joined and began her lessons with me and slowly replaced the first teacher entirely. Both of these teachers were native Uzbeks, who spoke only in Russian during our lessons and occasionally boasted of achievements of the Soviet System since the end of the Second World War. They narrated about sacrifices of the Soviet people during the war, which forced survived soldiers, already married before, to marry widows of their fallen colleagues.

Teachers and officials in the University and people outside it in the city were generally cordial. Conversations of foreigners with the locals always started in a volley of standard questions in the same sequence: "Where are you from?", "How are you called?", "What are you doing here?", "How do you like here?, and, after hearing responses to these questions from the visitor, there were frequent comments like: "Nehru, Raj Kapoor", "We are friends.", and "You speak Russian well." irrespective of the visitor's command of this language perhaps not to discourage him/her from speaking in it. At the time of departure after the conversation, there used to be a standing invitation from the locals in the form: "Come down to us." A visitor unfamiliar with ceremonial courtesy of conversation of this kind wondered how to reach the inviting local without knowing his/her address. I was a witness of such an invitation for the first time when an elderly lady incidentally engaged with us in a conversation during a journey in tramway invited us just before she was about to get down from it.

It was a great surprise for me to know that there were always a couple of tables reserved for foreigners in hotel restaurants close to their entrances. I gathered this wealth of knowledge during a reception accorded in the restaurant of the leading city hotel by Foreign Affairs Section to an Indian official from National Council of Educational Research and Training (NCERT), who had come on a short trip to different institutions in the Soviet Union to prepare report on teaching curricula and textbooks in schools there. Like other distinguished guests, this visiting official was accommodated in this hotel. The waiter attending us

boasted of the information that Ráj Kapoor used to occupy
the adjoining table during inauguration of his films and,
once when asked whether he knew Russian, he retorted
that he only spoke Russian well. This was an apparent
reference to dubbed dialogues of his roles in the films shown
in the Soviet Union.

Some time later after my arrival I came to know three
compatriots: Arun Srivástava, Sultán Hamid and Sisodiá.
Arun was in the last stage of doing his candidate's dissertation in the field of growth of cotton in the local agriculture
institute, Sultán was doing some job in the film industry,
and Sisodiá was working in Tashkent Radio. Arun had
come from Bihár on a stipend and lived in a hostel. He
spoke in very sketchy Russian despite his long stay, but
his narration of different events in his life in Tashkent was
full of wit. Once he told that all letters that he sent to,
and received from, his family in Bihár were censored. To
support his assertion he cited an example of a letter that
he wrote in standard Hindi to his family describing the
common life in the Soviet Union, but he received back this
letter after some days with the remark from the sensors
that its language was filthy. However, Arun rewrote the
contents of the letter in Bhojpuri dialect, and this time the
letter reached his family unhindered.

I felt that Arun was a great friend of Sultán, who had his
own apartment which I visited a couple of times to spend
some time together. I learnt that Sultán was an assistant
to the famous film director, Mahboob Khán, of Mother
India, and came with him to promote this film in the Soviet
Union. Here Sultán met a young Russian girl connected
with the film industry and decided to live with her here.
To do so, he renounced his Indian citizenship to take Soviet

citizenship. However, things did not go smoothly with them and, after their divorce, he settled in Tashkent. Sisodiá was probably a member of the Communist Party of India and was employed in Tashkent Radio as a news broadcaster for the Indian audience. He read news in Hindi, with his characteristic UP-style accent, every evening.

I met Ahmed first in the Foreign Affairs Section. He had come from Dháká in Bangládesh. Like many others, he too got a stipend to do his master's degree. He lamented that he left his Bachelor's studies half-way in Dháká and had to begin his master's studies here again with a loss of two years. He was a practising Muslim and suspected that he was under constant watch of some spying agency. He was very unhappy. Loud music played from the parallel wing of his U-shaped hostel, opposite his room, was additionally detrimental to his psyche. Unlike Ahmed, Mohammed Orazov lived in my hostel where persons doing their candidate's studies and short-term visitors with higher qualifications had been accommodated. He was from Ashkhabad State University, Turkmenistan, and was doing his candidate's degree in mathematics. He was always there to help me in various ways including guiding to the city for sightseeing and purchases.

Schedule of lessons with the Russian language and pressure of adjustment with the new surroundings, hampered by insufficient communication capabilities, kept me so busy in the initial period of stay that I considered it unwise to demand from the Foreign Affairs Section access to the laboratory for my research work. However, in the beginning of the new year of 1975 when I learned of normal lessons on socialist economy being planned for me as well with the Egyptian students, I flatly refused to attend these planned lessons. I argued that I was a postdoctoral fellow rather than a student for some degree and that I had come to do research work. In view of my insistence on knowing my actual status, Foreign Affairs Section organized a visit to the Physics Department of the University. During the visit I was disappointed to discover that they were doing some work on electrical conductivity of solids. This work was of no specific relevance to my research activities. Immediately after the visit I bluntly told the Foreign Affairs Section that I was merely wasting time there and nothing was there for me to do. I insisted that they wrote to the USSR Ministry of Education in Moscow with specific information that work of my interest was being carried out in the Institute of Crystallography, Moscow, and in the Leningrad University. They indeed wrote to the Ministry of Education as I had wanted. Mr Rustamov's smile of welcome to my frequent visits to the Foreign Affairs Section was a great consolation in this endurance. Rustamov was roughly of my age.

Bureaucracy is a process that tests the patience of those who come across it and I was one of its victims to wait for a long period of some three months to receive a decision of change of institution from the Ministry of Education. I did not sit idle then but, based on the research material that I had brought with me, prepared manuscripts of papers for publication in different journals. The Foreign Affairs Section proved very helpful in getting the number of typed copies of my texts required by editorial offices of the prospective journals, but there was a problem with preparing copies of each of the photographs that I had with me. Fortunately, then I met an American journalist who had arrived for a couple of months on some stipend in Tashkent and lived in the same hostel where I was living. She had come to pursue research work for her PhD dissertation on the connection between Central Asian languages and the ancient Turkish language and to prepare photographic and phonic documentation for this purpose. During our conversation about our past and present activities when I told that I needed copies of photographs, she offered her services, which enabled me to publish three papers in different known journals, even two of them in Russian-language journals translated by their Editorial Offices from my original English texts. However, I regret now that I did not acknowledge then my gratefulness to her in any of these papers.

Finally, when a response from the Ministry of Education about my relocation reached the University authorities, they informed me immediately, but I was disappointed to know that the new placement was in Baku State University instead of the two options I had wanted. The University authorities expressed their helplessness in the matter and, following the directive from the Ministry, began to make arrangements for my journey to Baku, but they expressed the opinion that I visit Samarkand and Bukhara before that journey. I accepted this suggestion and the Foreign Affairs Section planned two separate trips to Samarkand and Bukhara by plane. In Samarkand I was a guest of Samarkand University where a small group of students of the English language, headed by their teacher, tested with me their conversational capabilities for two days and guided me to see important sites in the city. Trip to Bukhara by airflight was with a transit at Samarkand. During this trip to Bukhara I met at the Samarkand Airport a person who told that his family was of Indian origin and were trapped in Uzbekistan at the time of October Revolution.

I was indeed impressed by many historical monuments like Kalyan Minaret, Bibi Khanum Mosque and Timur mausoleum, among others, in these cities.

After the above trips I landed in Baku University and it was already May. Here also I was accommodated in one of the University hostels, where mainly foreigners resided. Foreign Affairs Section of the University was also located in this hostel. In the main hall of the hostel at the entrance where a porter, frequently a middle-aged fattish lady, kept watch of visitors to hostel inhabitants and verified the presence of inhabitants in the rooms from room-keys held on systematically arranged upward bent nail-like hooks fixed into the wooden keyboard hanging on the wall nearby. In the hall I also noticed, on its wall, a list of countries of students studying in the University and colourful sculptures of left and right parts of open books carved by their side. After my arrival, India was added to the existing list of countries of students.

Soon after my arrival to Baku I approached the Foreign Affairs Section and demanded that I should know what I would do in Baku. Deputy Secretary of this Section, Comrade Ivanovskii, was responsible for these matters. Perhaps he was older than me by a couple of years. I learned that he hailed from Ukrainian Soviet Socialist Republic. It was an open secret in those days that members of local structures of the Communist Party occupied all prominent positions in various organizations, such as sections and departments in a university, but deputies to secretaries of all prominent positions in Central Asian and Caucasian Republics were ethnic Russians. This policy was so perhaps due to the belief of the central administration that local officials in the republics were not so sincere in realizing the socialist ideology and the ethnic Russian deputies acted as the real driving force in reaching this goal in different ways.

Some days later Ivanovskii informed me that a date had been fixed for my visit to the Physics Department and its Head would wait for me to explain about the scientific activities being carried out there. Following the instructions passed on to me, I reached the Department on the appointed day. The meeting there was cordial, but I found that they had been investigating semiconducting properties of elemental semiconductors and, in one of the corner of their laboratory, they had a home-made horizontal furnace for the growth of these semiconductor crystals. I was not interested in this type of investigations and thanked the hosts for their courtesy. This was another disappointment that I met.

Immediately after my visit to the Physics Department of the University, I reported the situation to the Foreign Affairs Section and requested them to inform the USSR Ministry of Education in Moscow that there was nothing for me in Baku State University and I needed relocation as explained in the previous letter of my transfer from the Tashkent State University. They also did as I wanted and I began to wait for the response from Moscow.

In the hostel lived, among others, Noor Mohammed, a young boy from Kandhar Province of Afghanistan, doing his Masters' studies. He drew my attention due to the fact that he spoke in Hindi well. When I asked the reason of proficiency of his Hindi, he narrated that, as a child, he stayed for some time in Bombay, the present-day Mumbai, with his uncle who had been doing business of dry fruits there. Apart from this, he watched many Bollywood movies frequently shown in cinema-halls in Afghanistan. His narration was genuine because, from my own experience with the two sons of one of my non-Gujaráti friends in Gujarát, I knew that children grasp new languages very fast. Still I remember Noor for his sober composure and affectionate attitude.

In Baku I had a lot of free time which I availed to know compatriots living there in other educational institutions and to visit important sites in the region. There I met Sitáraman who was doing his candidate's studies in the Technical University. He stayed in a hostel and we began to visit each other. Sitáraman's only problem was that he spoke poor Hindi and I had always been a staunch supporter of speaking in any Indian language common to both of us. Despite this handicap, we liked our companionship and frequently met each other. During one of our meetings I tauntingly commented what type of Indian he was that he did not speak in Hindi. He smilingly promised me that he would learn it.

I learned that there was a seventeenth century Fire Temple on the outskirts of Baku. I was amazed to find its resemblance with old Hindu temples, but I was highly fascinated by the sculptures written in Devanágari script on the temple walls in a language reminiscent of old form of Hindi encountered in Meerabái's songs. There were a few sculptures inscribed in Gurmukhi and Persian scripts. I also learned that Guru Nának Dev had stayed in this temple. It is indeed possible that the First Guru stayed here in this temple because a sizeable Hindu community of traders lived in Baku where he could expect them to follow his teachings. Moreover, Sikhism did not become a religion of large followers immediately from the first Guru. Sikhism took its form afterwards. Since Baku was situated on the Silk trade route from China to Middle East, this temple provided shelter to travellers and religious preachers during their journeys from, and to, India.

I remember Baku for plenty of fresh fruit in the bazaar, but many finished products, including garments, were scarce in supermarkets. Once I heard a middle-aged lady visitor from another Republic complaining that there was practically nothing in Baku, but she could buy everything in her city. I was also a witness of local patriotism during one of my purchasing spree in a supermarket when the lady at the paying counter uttered the amount "altmas" in Azerbaijani language and, when I requested her to give the amount in Russian, she quipped that I was expected to speak in Azerbaijani there instead of Russian. The issue was settled with the assistance of Noor Mohammed who wittily translated for me "altmas" into "forty" in Russian.

Armenia and Georgia border with Azerbaijan. Therefore, keeping in mind their proximity I expressed my desire to the Foreign Affairs Section to visit Tiblisi. They organized the visit by making arrangements of my travel by train and accommodation in a hostel in Tiblisi State University. In Tiblisi I met Bhattáchárya couple who had come there like me as postdoctoral fellows and had been staying in the same hostel where I had been accommodated. In Tiblisi I found Stalin's statues despite his public denunciation by the Communist Party and both young and old people participating in mass celebrations in Churches there though practising religion in the Soviet Union was forbidden.

It was the beginning of July already and there was no response from the Ministry of Education in Moscow about my transfer. Therefore, I requested the Foreign Affairs Section to arrange for my visit to the Ministry. After an initial unwillingness, finally they made arrangements of my entire visit to the Ministry in Moscow by plane and accommodation there. In the Ministry I explained to the lady attending my documents that I would prefer to go back to India if there were problems in transferring me to the Institute of Crystallography of the Academy of Sciences. During another meeting of this visit with the lady, she promised that a decision in this regard would be taken soon. With this promise I flew back to Baku.

Summer vacations were fast approaching and I had practically nothing to do in Baku. Therefore, I asked the Foreign Affairs Office to arrange for my vacations. With Ivanovskii I had good understanding and frequently talked with him on different issues related to my stay. During one of our conversations I suggested that they should show on the wall a decorated bed instead of the carved open book in the main hall alongside the list of countries of stipend holders for studies. Without uttering a word he simply smiled at the suggestion. Some days later he informed me that I would have my three-week vacations in Leningrad. I was relieved of the burden of spending vacations and that too in Leningrad which was one of my options to carry out my scientific work. Thus, equipped with railway tickets and other documents related to the contact persons and accommodation in Leningrad, I set out to spend my summer vacations at the end of the month.

Next day I reached Leningrad Central Railway Station in Moscow and a day later Moscow Central Railway Station in Leningrad, and from there to my destination of accommodation in a hostel. There I met Brij Mohan

Thákur, who had come from Simferopol to spend his vacations here. He hailed from the Terai Region of Nepál and had been studying medicine in a university in Simferopol in Crimea. We remained together in the group of vacationists accommodated in the hostel. There were also two Cubans: Roberto and Juan. Foreigners studying in different institutions in the western part of the Soviet Union mainly composed this group. Apart from visiting the fountains and gardens of Petergof and the school, where Pushkin received his elementary education, located on the outskirts of Leningrad, we had great time in watching the historical Ermitaż, Niva river and walking on the streets of the Leningrad itself during the white nights.

After the vacations I returned to Baku, where a communication from the Ministry of Education had been waiting for me. I was instructed to join the Institute of Crystallography in Moscow from the beginning of September and work with Aida Aleksandovna Urusovskaya in the Laboratory of Mechanical Properties. I was happy that ultimately I was going to work in the institution where I had intended to go long before when I applied for the fellowship. I wrote to Urusovskaya about my plans of arrival in Moscow.

In Moscow I was first accommodated in a hotel close to the centre of the city in the beginning of the Leninskii Prospekt (Lenin Avenue). Like many other well-known institutes specialized in different scientific fields, Institute of Crystallography was also situated on Leninskii Prospekt. Later I was shifted to a students' hostel not far from the Institute. There I stayed in a room with one ethnic Russian, with his family name Belykh, a thorough gentleman, who took care of me in the ensuing cold months. It was a great experience to join him in plugging unseen narrow slits in the window of the room by thrusting rolls of wool into them to minimize loss of heat from it in the severe winter period of Moscow. Students from different Soviet Republics and short-time visitors from countries of the Soviet Bloc lived in this hostel. The hostel residents frequently used the common kitchen on each floor to cook minor food items and boil water to prepare tea. These common kitchens were good meeting places for acquaintance. In the floor kitchen I came to know some students from Central Asian Republics of Kyrgyzstan and Tajikistan and from Mongolia. From the routine Soviet-style conversations when they learned my country of origin, some of them began to invite me for tea or "plov." One of them was Nuria Alybaeva, who was working for her candidate's degree in the Institute of Crystallography which I had joined recently. She hailed from Kyrgyzstan and had been living in the hostel with her cousin sister. I indeed relished their delicious plov cooked with freshly-purchased mutton in the bazaar they knew and native spices they had brought with them. But I was not comfortable in this hostel due to the prevalent noisy atmosphere.

I narrated my situation to Aida Aleksandrovna, as I usually addressed her. After some days I was allotted a furnished one-room flat on the tenth or eleventh floor of a block situated on the Gubkin street nearby. I lived in this flat until my departure.

Two groups of workers were engaged in the investigation of mechanical properties of crystals in the laboratory. One of these groups was headed by Galina Berezkova and the other by Aida Urusovskaya. Nuriya Alybaeva was doing her candidate's dissertation with Galina Berezkova, but Natasha Sizova, Elena Darinskaya and Alyosha Smirnov worked with Aida Urusovskaya. Natasha Sizova and Elena Darinskaya were senior workers holding candidate's degrees, but Alyosha Smirnov was working for his Candidate's dissertation and was an employee of the Institute. He used to write poetry. Galina Berezkova wrote a book on whisker crystals and this book was frequently cited in the literature on crystals published in the Soviet Union, but I never saw any reference to this book in the western literature published in English. The founder of the laboratory, Marina Klassen-Nekyudova, was now retired but frequently she used to come to the laboratory. Marina Klassen-Nekyudova had done pioneering work before on the plasticity of crystals and had worked with Academician Shubnikov, the founder of the Institute of Crystallography. The Chief of the Laboratory of Mechanical Properties at that time was Vladimir Govorkov, a young man who had completed his candidate's dissertation not long ago. When I wanted to know why a young man like Govorkov was the Laboratory Chief, I was told that he was an active member of the Party, but other senior workers were not its members. This laboratory was on the third floor, and one of the main instruments for measurements of deformation of single crystals was an Instron machine procured from the West.

I had known Aida Aleksandrovna's previous research work, carried out with Marina Klassen-Nekyudova and Thyágarájan, on the plastic deformation of lead sulphide crystals. Marina Klassen-Nekyudova was still active in this area with different workers in the laboratory. After completing his candidate's dissertation Thyágarájan joined Solid State Physics Laboratory affiliated to the Ministry of Defence in Delhi. When I was pursuing my PhD thesis

he was generous to gift me some lead sulphide crystals
for my investigations. I found that, apart from being a
good scientist, Aida Aleksandovna was an opera singer.
Once she gave brilliant feat of her opera performance in
the Institute with her younger sister on the occasion of
some festival.

I was accommodated to work on the first floor of the
Institute in the laboratory of Vasil Miuskov, who had been
studying defect structure of crystals using x-ray topography. Two middle-aged women worked in the laboratory
alternatively as assistants. I was given a table with several
shelves and an optical microscope. After a couple of days
of my settling down in the laboratory, Aida Aleksandrovna
asked me to give a seminar on my research activities and
entrusted me to find a non-poisonous solvent as replace-
ment of methanol for revealing dislocations in cesium iodide
crystals which she studied in early sixties. In the seminar I
concentrated on presenting experimental results of general
trends for devising suitable etching solutions for revealing
dislocations in solutions. The seminar was well received
and Marina Klassen-Nekyudova even commented that sadly
Chernov was not invited to attend that seminar. Marina's
comment indeed flattered me especially because I had not
met Aleksander Chernov before but I knew this name from
his publications on fundamental aspects of crystal growth.

I learned that Vasil Miuskov had worked before in UK
with A.R. Lang, one of the pioneers in x-ray topography.
He was the only one in the Soviet Union, who began to
study dislocation structure in crystals by x-ray topography
and was fascinated by the way of carrying out research
work in Lang's laboratory. From frequent conversations
with Vasil Miuskov I always felt his sense of sincerity to

what he was doing but gathered an impression that he was not happy with the organization of scientific life in the Soviet Union and the Soviet-made x-ray machine that he had for his work on the topography of crystals. Once he even quipped that the machine that he was using was a copy of Philips machines sold in the West.

One day Aida Aleksandrovna told me that a journalist was planning to write an article on the life of students and visitors in the Soviet Union and this journalist would visit the laboratory to have my photograph with her in connection with this article. On the appointed day the journalist came to the laboratory and took a couple of photographs where both of us held a plastic model of the shape of a crystal. I did not come across this article during my stay in Moscow, but on my return to India I came to see my photograph with the model of a crystal in an illustrated Soviet magazine, published in Hindi, gifted to my family in the countryside by a cloth merchant known to me.

I found the task of replacing methanol as a solvent for etching cesium iodide crystals not so difficult to realize. I indeed found many solvents, including ethanol, to replace it and documented my findings on photographic films which we used in those days. The ladies in the laboratory developed the films and, whenever I wanted, prepared prints on photographic papers. Based on these results we published two papers in two different journals. The manuscripts for submission to editorial offices of the journals were typed on a traditional typewriter imported from the German Democratic Republic.

I remained mainly in Miuskov's laboratory or in the main library. The library subscribed various foreign journals in English and original Russian-language journals, and had acquired books that I did not have access to before. The lady-librarians were always there to carry from the numerous library shelves heaps of journals and books to the table I had occupied before. There was no possibility of photocopies of printed material from books and journals in those days. Therefore, I tried to go through most of the relevant literature of my interest and made notes of important information in an exercise book that I purchased for this purpose. Majority of my notes dealt with experimental results published after the publication of Buckley's book in 1951 on the effect of different compounds on the shapes of crystals grown from solutions. The reason for this collection was my blurred, and unsubstantiated, vision of important role of small amounts of foreign compounds added to solutions of solutes resulting in crystals of different shapes during growth and in forming etch pits of different geometries on the faces of the crystals during dissolution. I had been dreaming of establishing some relationship between these shapes of crystals or geometries of dissolution figures and the chemical nature of the foreign compound in the solution.

I went to the laboratory on the third floor occasionally, where we discussed some urgent research problems and took tea prepared from popular elephant-brand tea-leaves imported from India. Sometimes the tea contained pure ethyl alcohol mixed with it in good proportion, from the bottles kept in a locked cupboard under the supervision of Aida Aleksandrovna, when some of the ladies politely asked her for it in cold winter days. Generally, we talked about research problems during our long walks with Elena Darinskaya to one of the restaurants of the Moscow State

University during lunch breaks. During one of such conversations I suggested that our observations of changes in the geometry of pits produced on the cubic faces of cesium iodide crystals by solutions of ethyl alcohol containing different copper chloride could be due to different copper complexes formed in the solutions and that identification of chemical structure of these complexes deserved due attention for this purpose. Aida Aleksandrova listened to my line of thoughts attentively and consulted some researchers in the Institute, who had been studying chemical structure of complexes in solutions. After some time we studied our solutions using ultraviolet-visible spectroscopy.

I did not understand why I had been accommodated in Miuskov's laboratory on the first floor instead of the laboratory of mechanical properties on the third floor. Congestion in the latter was the possible reason for this arrangement. Another reason that could be discerned was the general tendency of officials of different institutions in the Soviet Union to restrict access of foreign visitors to the actual state of the knowledge. Perhaps these officials did not want the visitors to become wiser than the hosts. In my case, I did not learn much about mechanical properties, but I learned much more than this loss by working in Miuskov's laboratory and making notes from the published literature in the Institute library independently.

Immediately after arriving in Moscow I went to the Indian Embassy to report my place of residence. The person-in-charge for these matters was the same who changed my twenty dollars into roubles at the official rate. I had known by now that the official dollar-to-rouble exchange rate was much lower than the black-market rate, where I could get some three to four times of roubles. Therefore, I told him to give me back my twenty dollars that I sold him one year ago. He returned my dollars and I handed him over the amount of roubles I got from him. Here in the Embassy I came to know that there were several young compatriots studying in the Moscow State University. They lived in the University hostels.

I was curious to meet some of the compatriots studying in the Moscow State University, and I indeed met some of them later. Among them I found good common language with Suresh Khanná and his close friend Jose. Suresh came from Punjab but Jose from Kerala. Suresh was doing his candidate's degree in Physics, and Jose studied Russian literature. I used to visit them frequently on free days to spend some time together and relish Indian-style dishes they cooked in their kitchens. Thanks to my visits there I met several other compatriots. Hindi was the common lingua franca of this group of compatriots who usually shared rooms in segments of two or three rooms with students of other nationalities. It was indeed internationalism there, where conversations of habitants of neighbouring rooms could easily be heard because their designers and constructors did not make the rooms sound-proof during their erection. Perhaps they were built so either to ensure transparent conduct of residents or to serve neighbours in following and knowing what was happening nearby. One of the compatriots once told that his neighbour from German Democratic Republic wanted to know from him the language of conversation between him and his friend that they had the previous day. When this compatriot told that it was Hindi, this neighbour responded that he could give the summary of the conversation. From the neighbour's response he realized that their conversation in Hindi contained too many English words, as has been the fashion in the Indian elite, embedded in it and the neighbour arranged these English words in a logical sequence to decipher the topic of conversation.

The lowest temperatures in the winters of my native countryside were spent under quilts in closed rooms, built mainly from sun-baked mud-bricks, and the sunrise outside was sufficient to warm our bodies and minds. I saw snow and snow-fall only in films in cinema halls. In sharp contrast to the life in my native countryside, winter in Moscow was really harsh and frequently it snowed in plenty. But communication by metro and tramways usually remained functional. Somewhere in January a friend paid me a visit to my flat. Late in the evening I accompanied him to the tramway stand to see him off when we had to wait for some time for the tram. Then we discovered that the temperature was even lower than minus thirty degrees Celsius.

Aida Aleksandrovna once invited me to spend some time on skiing in the vast fields of snow close to her apartment in the south of Moscow. Since I had never gone on skiing before, I gladly accepted her invitation and decided to experiment with this adventure. She explained that her apartment was located in a multi-storeyed building built not long ago on the outskirts of the city. On the fixed day I reached the destination where Aida and her husband Igor had been waiting for me with a spare pair of ski for my experiments. I was indeed overwhelmed by the snow lying there and the crowd of people enjoying its presence in different ways.

After binding my pair of ski on my feet with the assistance of my hosts, I tried my unknown skill of moving

over the snow. The result of these attempts was biting
off the snow a couple of times until I reached the modest
conclusion of making no more efforts to become an object
of fun for grown-up participants who were skiing freely or
for youngsters playing with the snow either by throwing
snow-balls on each other or by collecting heaps of snow to
build snowmen. I had nobody to throw snow-balls at but
observed snowmen in the making in our neighbourhood.
Inspired by these works, I began to collect snow for large
balls to erect a snowman. With the joint efforts of my hosts
my rudimentary three-part snowman finally developed into
a pleasing sculpture. Some time later our snowman drew
the attention of a local journalist who took its photograph
and came to know in person its artists. I was happy with
this short-lived achievement which I never tried again.

A retired professor from Jawáharlál Nehru University,
popularly known by its acronym JNU, in Delhi lived with
his wife and young pregnant daughter in one of the apartments a couple of floors above my apartment. He had come
to Moscow on a stipend to do some research work on Nehru.
It was somewhat mysterious for me why this professor was
doing this research on Nehru here in Moscow, but, from the
general leftist tendency of teachers and students of JNU,
I believed that he was somehow connected with the Communist Party of India. I never enquired from him where
precisely he was doing his research work, but I observed
that his wife frequently went for shopping to grocery stores,
popularly known as 'magazins' there, and returned with
heavy bags of purchases in both of her hands. I used to
visit them and did not even mind doing some shopping
for them in the shops where I did my own purchases of
food stuff. From my own experience of movement in the

slippery streets during the winter in Moscow, I was convinced that this old professor couple needed such support. I always remembered that once I suffered from hip pain for several days after I fell down by slipping on a freshly snowed footpath close to the Institute while returning to my apartment.

Spring brought different news and witnessed new events. During a visit to my neighbour Professor's apartment, he told that one of his books on Nehru had been published. He showed his book and some reviews on its contents. The book was published by a publisher in Delhi. His daughter received a visa to travel to US to join her husband. An early travel was planned so that she could deliver her child there. In any case, I did not understand then the riddle of praise of socialist system by the professor and haste of travel to the capitalist US by his pregnant daughter. Perhaps the learned professor knew that socialist ideology and well-being do not go hand in hand.

It was joyful to go for purchases in magazins (grocery shops) during spring when clients could stand outside a magazin in a queue to purchase some much-needed product. Once I stood in a queue before a magazin specialized in alcohol drinks to buy a bottle of vodka. The person following me began to show immense intimacy. After traditional introductory exchanges of questions and answers related to my country of origin, my activities here, duration of stay, and good friendship between the two countries, this man asked me politely whether I could contribute some kopeykas (coins) to the amount he was possessing with him to buy a beer. I smiled at his friendliness and gave a couple of coins which he gladly slipped into his pocket with customary words of gratefulness.

In the case of occasional shortage of some food items, such as onions or potatoes, in the Moscow magazins, I found that foreigners could buy them without standing in queues. I made this discovery when I was in need of potatoes which were being sold in a magazin with a long queue of clients patiently waiting for their turn to buy a fixed weight of 3 kilos of potatoes per client. When I caught the tail of the queue, I was advised by the persons standing before me to buy 'my potatoes' without standing in the queue. I did so and went to my apartment. Immediately thereafter, I went to the Professor's apartment to enquire whether they had potatoes. Unfortunately, they did not have, and I took the responsibility of buying potatoes for them as well and reached the same magazine again. When I stood before the gate of the magazin, the lady controlling the entrance of clients from the queue let me in unhindered. This time the disposer of potatoes asked me how much potatoes I needed. Unsure of whether he was not joking, I muttered "5 kilos." But he said in his routine "Khorosho" (Russian equivalent of "Well") and weighed 5 kilos of potatoes, which I gleefully carried to the Professor's apartment immediately in the bag they had given me before.

I observed occasional dearth of some food items in the magazins in the neighbourhood of my flat. A handy explanation for these situations was that Soviet Union helped various countries across the Globe in different ways and consequently Soviet citizens experienced such shortages. During one of my visits to the hostel where I had stayed before, I heard this argument in a meeting of friends in Nuriya's room. Incidentally, this visit coincided with the days of rumour of import of onions from India. Since trade agreements between Soviet Union and other countries were bilateral, I silenced their argument that I heard from them by saying that nothing was free and every help was returned in the form of items like onions that they acquired recently from India. In our discussions afterwards I did not hear such arguments.

One could frequently hear about efforts of the Soviet Union in achieving peace in the World both in general public debate. One could frequently see in television broadcasts some Romesh Chandra, President of World Peace Council, talking about peace. I never heard of this name in India before my arrival in the Soviet Union nor did I hear of him later on my return. I noted enormous expression of sympathy with the Indians when a disaster in an American chemical plant in Bhilai resulted in the loss of the life of its workers. This sympathy could be due to two reasons. First, it happened in an American company; second, this tragedy occurred to Indians, their friends.

In the spring season when the temperature steadily rose with the passage of days, Mr and Mrs Bhattáchárya from Tiblisi and Sitáraman from Baku planned to see Moscow. The Bhattácháryas enjoyed cooking of fish and rice, but they equally relished eggs in different forms. Sitáraman surprised me with his conversation in Hindi, and commented that all this was thanks to me. He was not at all demanding regarding food, but always had his breakfast in the morning after taking a shower. He was too religious unlike most of other compatriots.

Suresh finished the experimental work on optical properties of crystals for his candidate's dissertation under the supervision of Boris Strukov. After the final defence of his thesis, he hosted a dinner for the members of his examination committee in my apartment. One of them was Lev Shuvalov, Editor-in-Chief of the journal "Kristallografiya" published in the Institute of Crystallography. I had heard of him before but knew him personally only during this dinner.

At the end of June 1976 Arun came to Moscow to obtain his candidate's degree (equivalent to PhD) in English from the Ministry of Education. After a period of over three years he defended his dissertation on the cultivation of cotton in Tashkent. I accompanied him to the Ministry. I was somewhat disgusted to find that he had difficulty in communicating with the lady official in the Ministry in "his" Russian. Although I never pretended that I knew better Russian, I was helpful in obtaining his degree from the Ministry. I gathered an impression from talks with him that he was not satisfied with the results of yield of cotton and level of irrigation of the crops mentioned in his thesis. He was convinced that these results were not reliable. In any case, equipped with his degree he left the Land of Soviets for home.

Summer vacations were fast approaching. I had been dreaming of spending them somewhere in the Baltic Republics. I expressed my wish to Aida Aleksandrovna, and she tried to arrange my vacations under the framework of workers of the Academy of Sciences. She encountered insurmountable barriers in this undertaking to the extent that, being my caretaker in the Institute, she faced the risk of not going on her vacations without organizing mine because I was not a worker of the Academy. According to the Academy, I was a stipend holder of the Ministry of Education and, therefore, the Ministry had to arrange for my vacations. Finally, Aida Aleksandrova informed me that my summer vacations for 21 days had been arranged in Moldavia with the students of Patrice Lumumba International Friendship University in Moscow. Now I felt that she could go on vacations with clean conscience.

I reached the assigned hostel of the Patrice Lumumba University in the early morning of the day of departure on vacations. I discovered there some 40-50 students of different nationalities and sexes. From there we went in buses to the Central Railway Station to board a train to Kishinev via Kiev. We reached Kiev at night. From Kishinev we went by buses to our destination located close to a small village. Our destination was an independent entity composed of a wide complex of rooms for the accommodation of guests like us who had come to have their vacations, a big kitchen with an attached dining hall, playgrounds for football and volleyball, and an open-air theatre for different performances.

Among the group of vacationists, apart from me there were 3 persons from India, one from Uttar Pradesh, one from Maháráshtra and one from Kerala. There were 5 persons from Pákistán, two from Punjáb, one from Sindh, one from Balochistán and one from the Pákistán-occupied part of Jammu and Kashmir (J&K). I observed that the vacationist from Balochistán did not mingle with his colleagues from Punjáb and Sindh, and the vacationist from J&K did not recognize that he represented Pákistán. There was no problem of this type with the Indian vacationists. However, despite coming from different countries I found excellent common language with the vacationists, Asgar and Hassan, from Punjáb, and Arif, from Sindh. We used to spend most of our time together. Usually, we talked in Punjábi but Arif spoke in Hindustani (or Urdu). Arif told that he understood Punjábi but did not speak in it. During a conversation he told that his parents had migrated from Uttar Pradesh at the time of partition. I observed that their greetings with the other compatriots from Balochistán and Pákistáni part of J&K were very casual.

Asgar, Hassan, Arif and I usually had walks after lunch and supper. Occasionally, we visited a house in the village nearby to try local grape-wine. For us such visits offered opportunities to know the village life in this part of the Soviet Union, but our hosts could also add a couple of roubles to their earnings in the summer season. Sometimes during our strolls we talked on various topics including politics, but we never used offensive words during our conversations. Once I heard from Arif that the common citizen was the victim of political whims of the leaders in our countries. He cited the example of purchase of some locomotive engines for Pákistán Railways from Germany at prices several times higher than those which could be purchased from India. He also lamented that there was poor trade of essential commodities between the two coun-tries, which was the reason of exorbitant prices of some of them in Pákistán. I did not ask these friends the fields of their studies, but Arif's observations convinced me that he was studying economics, although this could be socialist economy in his Patrice Lumumba University in those days.

In the last days of our vacations there, a cultural pro-gramme was organized in the open-air theatre. An excellent dancing performance was given by Sri Lankan girl-students. We four gave a bhangrá performance, and, thanks to those friends, that bhangrá dance was the only one in which I participated in my life. To fill the programme I also performed a song from the film "Padosan" (Lady neighbour), but my song was not the only one in this event.

After returning from the vacations I concentrated on winding up my stay in the Institute. During this period of long and warm days I noted that "subbotniks" were commonly organized in the Institute practically every Saturday. The name subbotnik finds its roots in the Russian word "subbota" for "Saturday", which was a free day in all government institutions in those days. I decided to participate in one of the subbotniks when workers from the Institute used to clean the compound outside its main building from paper bits, stray grass, leaves from the trees and dust. My participation had dual purpose: to know how these subbotniks were organized and functioned, and to show that I was also one of the workers of the Institute. Following the programme hanging in the Institute notice-board, I reached the meeting place where the participants began to work using spades, brooms, dustpans, handcarts and pointed sticks. I took a broom and began to collect leaves scattered here and there while others became engaged in other tasks. After a couple of hours I noticed one of the workers of the Institute taking photographs of participants in the subbotnik. At this moment I saw Vladimir Govorkov appearing from nowhere and standing with a broom before the photographer. I was somewhat surprised to note this act of Vladimir because I did not see him before participating in the subbotnik. Some days later after the subbotnik I happened to go to the laboratory on the third floor. I saw there, on the notice-board, different photographs of several workers from the laboratory, but Vladimir Govorkov's pictures were most prominent among them. I smiled at this distinction for Vladimir and attributed it to his leading role in the community of the Institute as a member of the Communist Party.

Some days before the date of my departure I went to Baltona supermarket to buy different presents for my family and for my friends. This supermarket was situated in the neighbourhood of the hotel where I spent my first days on my arrival to Moscow two years ago. On my way to the restaurant of the hotel after the purchase of presents, it was a big surprise for me to meet the same young blond guide who received me at the airport two years ago. After these two years he had put on sufficient weight which made him appear manly and somewhat sluggish. He told that he had climbed up in the party hierarchy.

I wound up my stay in Moscow by disposing of all articles that could not be accommodated in the allowed luggage in my flight to Pálam Airport in Delhi. At the Airport after the passport control, a customs officer, who happened to be a lady in her early thirties, thoroughly checked items contained in my bags and informed me that for most of them I was to pay customs' duties. I argued that I had returned after two years, but the lady remained unmoved and gave the address where I could pay the duties. Thereafter, I picked up my luggage, came out of the airport and hired a taxi to reach the residence quarter of my friend Vijay in Old Delhi.

January 2022

4

AMIDST COMRADES

HE WAS BORN A TINY VILLAGE in the old Lublin Voivode-ship of the forty-nine voivodeships, organizational units, something like districts in India and prefectures in Japan, of the People's Republic of Poland, popularly known by its acronym PRL from the Polish name of the country, some-where in the early fifties of the nineteenth century. Those were the days of deep socialism in the country governed by the Polish United Workers' Party, known by the acronym PZPR from its Polish name, farmers inheriting chunks of land from their parents were dubbed 'kułaks' and their chil-dren were not easily enrolled for higher education and were refused accommodation in students' hostels, and members of the Party enjoyed privileges of preferred recruitment of their wards for higher education and special coupons for al-lotment of living flats from government-controlled housing societies. The outcome of this policy was that there were people who became members of the Party and availed of the benefits flowing from accepting the leading role of the only 'dutiful Party' and began to participate in the May-day parades organized by it. And our Bernard Marciniak, popularly addressed as "Bienek" by his colleagues, from the tiny village was not an exception.

After completing his school education Bienek joined Warsaw University of Technology (in Polish: Politechnika Warszawska) for his master's degree in chemistry. It was here during this period that he became an ardent worker of the Party. As soon as he received his master's degree in the early seventies, he was directed to strengthen the teaching staff of the newly established Pedagogical College in Częstochowa. As per his academic qualification, he joined the College as an assistant, equivalent of a junior lecturer, of chemistry in the Faculty of Mathematics and Natural Sciences.

In the sixties there were hardly ten full-fledged universities in Poland, but in many cities there were professional schools which trained candidates for jobs of teachers in schools and engineers in factories. The Party had its own ambitions. The existing universities were reorganized by splitting them in usual and professional agricultural and medical academies. The responsibility of reorganization of these institutions was entrusted to professors or docents having allegiance to the Party. There were many Jewish-origin Polish nationals occupying high positions in them. However, when USA and its allies adopted the policy to support the newly-founded State of Israel and the Soviet Union and its allies to support Arab countries during the Israel-Arab conflict, the Party intensified its doubts on the allegiance of Jewish-origin Polish nationals to PRL. Sensing the prevailing atmosphere of insecurity and the Party's policy to relieve them from positions held by them, many of them left the country in the late sixties. This resulted in a deficiency of highly qualified teaching staff in these universities. To make up this gap the Ministry of Higher Education promoted all employees having doctoral degrees to the posts of "docents" (pronounced: dotsents), equivalent to readers or associate professors in the universities of anglo-saxon countries. These promotions suddenly made them qualified to become independent or self-contained workers, to supervise research work of fresh doctoral candidates, and, among them, members of the Party were appointed directors of institutes and deans of faculties.

In early seventies the Party decided to set up independent pedagogical institutions of higher education, usually called "wyższe szkoły" equivalent of colleges, in the capital of every voivodeship, which did not have an institution of higher learning. The task of organization of each of these colleges was entrusted to individual members of the hard core of the Party, and one of the existing professional schools in the capital of a voivodeship was upgraded to the college. In Częstochowa the already functioning Teachers' Training School was transformed to the Pedagogical College, and Comrade Marian Jakubowski was deputed as its first Rector from Warsaw by the Party High Command to organize the College. He was a newly appointed docent in this College and had a doctoral degree in history or political philosophy.

From today's perspective recruitment of teaching staff for a college in an obscure place far off from known cities was indeed a challenge, but three factors facilitated this undertaking. The first factor was Party's centralized structure streaming down from Warsaw to the lowest organization level with the first secretary of the Party communicating directly with the first secretaries in the capitals of voivodeships, who, in their turn, could communicate decisions of the Party to the secretaries at the lowest level. The second factor was that the voivodeship administration considered the setting up of a college as a matter of prestige and assured every assistance to the freshly designated rector of the college. Consequently, the recruited staff of the college could count on residential accommodation from new housing cooperatives that began to crop up, under the supervision of Party members, to build living apartments for the citizens employed, and to be employed in future, in government administration, factories or production cooperatives. The last factor was qualified candidates leaving annually existing universities in big cities and seeking employment in new colleges, which ensured them accommodation to plan family life at the very outset of their careers.

The College in Częstochowa began to function with two faculties. Students were enrolled for master's degrees in physics, chemistry and mathematics in the Faculty of Mathematics and Natural Sciences, and in the fields of basic education, philology of Polish, Russian and German languages, socialist economy and Marxist philosophy in the Faculty of Humanities and Pedagogy. Candidates for the recruitment of the teaching staff were mainly from Jagiellonian University in Cracow (in Polish 'Kraków') and University of Wrocław. For example, soon after obtaining his master's degree in Chemistry from Cracow, Janusz Kliś was engaged to work as an assistant and, at the time of his selection, Rector Jakubowski informed him that he would live in one of the apartments on the third floor of the four-storeyed housing block just across the road opposite to his Office on Aleja Zawadzkiego, now known as ulica Armii Krajowej (National Army street). This housing block was on the verge of completion at that time. The Jakubczyks, Mieczysław and Ewa, who had completed their master's studies in Wrocław, were similarly selected to work as assistants in the Faculty of Mathematics and Natural Sciences. They were allotted an apartment in one of the new multi-storeyed housing blocks about one km away to the south of the College. Two doctorate holders, Natalia Zelichowicz and Bogdan Całusiński, working in the nearby technical college in the city, were engaged, as docents, to organize teaching for chemistry and physics students. Dr Ginalski, promoted to docent's position, was to organize teaching of mathematics. Teaching staff recruited later was not so fortunate to possess living accommodations immediately when they were selected, but they were promised to have independent houses. Henryk Kołodziej and Wojciech Lenkow, who studied in the University of Wrocław, were such employees. However, despite every effort of the college leadership, there were not many candidates for positions of "normal professors", who could establish future directions of research activities of its new employees. In fact, dearth of this independent teaching staff for most of the subjects persisted for decades after the inauguration of the College. But it continued functioning by engaging independent teaching staff from universities and research institutes of the Academy of Sciences situated in neighbouring cities, who travelled by trains to Częstochowa, frequently every second week for a couple of days, to rattle off their accumulated teaching lessons of the courses of a semester. There were also some of them who took under their wings assistants willing to carry out research work for doctoral degrees.

In early nineteen eighties the College could boast of merely three additions to the Faculty of Mathematics and Natural Sciences on permanent basis. One of them was Wanda Śliwa, a full-fledged professor with specialization in organic chemistry, who joined from the University of Wrocław. After some years she became Vice-Rector of the College and was responsible for scientific affairs. Eugeniusz Gurgul was another. He was appointed as a docent in chemistry and became a Director of the Institute of

Chemistry. He specialized in biochemistry and obtained a habilitation degree after his doctorate. He worked earlier in Szczecin (pronounced 'Shchechin'). As expected from top administrators, both Śliwa and Gurgul were members of the Party. Then there was Józef Świątek, pronounced as Yuzef Shwiontek, a docent, who was Director of the Institute of Physics. He studied thin films of organic compounds, and worked earlier in the Institute of Physics in Łódź University of Technology (Politechnika Łódzka, in Polish), but in early eighties left it immediately after obtaining his habilitation degree.

Józef Świątek left Łódź because the ruling so-called independent cadre lingered on dispatch of relevant documents to the Ministry of Higher Education for approval of his promotion to docent's position in the Institute. The reason of this attitude was simple. The ruling cadre, comprising three or four docents without habilitation degrees, sensed a threat to their position in the Institute, because docents with habilitation degrees had a higher status than theirs despite long services but with just doctorate degrees. They had been promoted previously to the positions of docents at the turn of nineteen sixties and seventies. However, Józef Świątek did not turn out to be loser in this move of his senior cadre of docents. Instead, in Częstochowa he inherited a group of young assistants to supervise their research for their doctoral degrees, first became a Director of the Institute of Physics and some years later a Dean of the Faculty of Mathematics and Natural Sciences, and was allotted an apartment in one of the housing blocks under construction on the outskirts of the city. According to the policy of the Government an employee could own only one apartment or house in those days, and it was a rarity to own an independent apartment for young people in big cities like Łódź. Józef had an apartment in Łódź. Therefore, he transferred the ownership rights of his apartment in Łódź to his elder daughter who was adult at that time.

In the nineteen eighties the Military Technical Academy (now called Military University of Technology) in Warsaw had been organizing, in Jurata, biannual scientific meetings on problems related to preparation and properties of solid and liquid crystals for researchers working in different institutions in Poland. After shifting to Poland in the nineteen eighty, I also began to participate in these meetings as one of the participants from the Institute of Physics, Łódź University of Technology. I joined this Institute as an adjunct professor (adiunkt, in Polish), equivalent to the post of an assistant professor or a lecturer according to the Anglo-Saxon system. When I joined the Institute, Józef Świątek had been finalizing his departure from it to Częstochowa.

Józef Świątek regularly attended the above biannual meetings in Jurata as an independent worker. He was accompanied by younger colleagues from his College presented results of their research work. One of these younger colleagues was Bienek, whom I happened to meet there for the first time. From the results that he presented I learned that he grew crystals of simple organic compounds from the vapour phase in long glass tubes. He impressed me by his efforts of growing good crystals in a practically unknown institution in the Country as well as by his modesty.

I came to know that he had obtained his doctorate degree some years ago under the supervision of Docent Włocławek, who somehow did not see himself working in future in Częstochowa and left for Opole. After Docent

Włocławek had left Częstochowa, Józef became Bienek's adviser in scientific matters. With time I also came to know that Bienek was holding the position of the first secretary of the Party Unit in the College. Sometime later I learned that he had advanced to the Party Executive at the Voivodeship level.

Despite leaving his previous working place in Łódź, Józef Świątek frequently visited it. There he came to know that I was preparing for my habilitation degree to become an independent worker. At that time my research work was more concentrated on processes of crystallization. Problems of this research were similar to that of Bienek and some of his colleagues in the Institute of Chemistry in the Faculty of Mathematics and Natural Sciences. In view of this, I was invited to visit them to find out something common for future collaboration.

On a mutually agreed day I travelled to Częstochowa from Łódź by a fast train. Bienek received me at the railway station and, after the visit, came to see me off. He indeed showed enormous zeal in carrying my small bag for my overnight stay there during the visit. In the College I met different people with unusual warmth and some of them even invited me to work with them.

Somewhere in the middle of nineteen eighty-six the Central Qualification Commission for evaluation of scientific output of candidates concurred with the decision of the Faculty of Physics, Chemistry and Mathematics of the University of Łódź for the award of habilitation degree in Experimental Physics to me. After receiving this information the ruling elite of my Institute was supposed to set up the procedure of my promotion to the position of a docent in the Institute. However, this elite showed utter negligence in this matter until the end of the year. I heard rumours that there were ideological hindrances in my promotion. The argument advanced in this connection was that I was not the right person to teach students because I hailed from a capitalistic country. In this period I received frequent telephone calls from Bienek of an offer to work in Częstochowa. But with enormous patience I waited for a favourable move of the ruling elite of the Institute for my promotion.

On the New Year's Eve I came to the Institute somewhat late. Docent Antony Drobnik, the then Director of the Institute, saw me and asked me to meet him in his office. He was a member of the Party and was one of those who were promoted to the posts of docents, without habilitation degrees, in early seventies. In his office he informed me of his expectations of my work in the Institute. He wanted that, as an adiunkt engaged in scientific research alone, I register my presence in the Institute and record time whenever I go out and return. When I enquired whether I was to register times of my visits to the central library and to the toilets, he howled at me that I was talking with a Polish director. I imagined then that he was still in Nigeria where he had worked in one of the universities or colleges at the turn of seventies and eighties on a yearly contract under some agreement between the Governments of Poland and Nigeria. He had pronounced in the Institute that he worked there in Nigeria on the post of a professor and had an official car and a driver, but he was not a professor at home. Having heard his pestering connotation of greatness, I retorted: 'For me it is practically impossible to work in the Institute in this way.' and wished him 'Good bye'. After my meeting with the Director, I called Bienek and informed him of my decision to work in Częstochowa. He arranged my meeting with Docent Edward Polanowski, the then Rector of the College, on January 2.

I came to know later that members of the Party were given preference to work on contracts in foreign countries in those days. These contractual workers were reliable plugs in their working places to collect relevant information about foreigners living or working in those countries for communication to security cell in the Party in Warsaw and were steady sources of earning hard currency from their salaries abroad for the state exchequer.

I reached the Main Railway Station in Częstochowa on January 2 by boarding an early morning express train. Bienek received me there and we sauntered to the entrance of the main building of the College on Zawadzki Avenue. As before during my earlier visits to Częstochowa, Bienek was generous again to pick my bag from me. The Rector's Office was situated on the first floor of this building. Rector Polanowski had been waiting for us there. The First Secretary of the Party unit of the College, Comrade Korbut, was also present. Bienek introduced us. In the meeting the Rector offered me to work as a docent from February itself and promised an accommodation immediately. He also informed that he would initiate the process of my transfer to Częstochowa from Łódź on the basis of mutual agreement with my employer. Since Bienek's research work was similar to mine, I accepted the proposal of joining the Department of Physical Chemistry, Bienek's working place in the Institute of Chemistry. After the meeting I returned to Łódź.

Somewhere in mid January someone from the Secretariat of the Institute informed me that Professor Kroh,

Rector of the University, wanted to see me. On the appointed hour I appeared in his Office. Rector Kroh told that he had received a letter from Częstochowa regarding my desire to undertake work there and enquired why I wanted to leave and whether I could continue to work in the present Institute and reach some understanding with the Director Drobnik. I explained my position and asserted: 'I have given a word to the Rector in Częstochowa and now I cannot back out.'. He pondered awhile and said: "I understand you." Then he wished me good luck. I still remember his composed and benign face when he uttered these last couple of sentences.

I joined the College in Częstochowa from February 1 and began to live in a two-room segment in the students' hostel nearby. Somewhere at the end of February the Ministry of Higher Education approved my promotion to the post of docent there.

When the news of Rector Kroh's acceptance of my final decision to leave the Institute reached the Director, unexpectedly he offered me to work on one-half post there. Keeping in view my scientific collaboration with some of the colleagues, including two younger colleagues working for their doctoral degrees under my supervision, I availed of this offer until summer vacations. However, attitude of the ruling elite of those docents was certainly not affable to me during this period.

Being an independent worker I became a member of the councils of the Institute, the Faculty and the College Senate. My participation in the meetings of these councils enabled me to become familiar with the functioning of the College and the academic status of its staff. Some of the members of its staff, especially in chemistry, were indeed of high academic stature, but a large number of them were in the budding stage. Publications in the English language, as a rule, appeared with the authors' affiliation as 'Pedagogical University of Częstochowa'. Justification for using the word "University" in the English-language publications by its authors, instead of the English equivalent "College" for "Wyższa Szkoła", was perhaps associated with the fact that it awarded master's degrees to its students, as in the case of traditional universities, after the completion of their studies. However, affiliation of publications in Polish always appeared with the original Polish name "Wyższa Szkoła." Its equivalent was also used in papers by authors from the Faculty of Humanities and Pedagogy in journals published in non-English languages in other countries such as German Democratic Republic, popularly known as East Germany with the acronym GDR or DDR. Since I had been publishing most of my scientific work in English, I began to publish my papers with the affiliation of Pedagogical University of Częstochowa. Since my research work was mainly focused on the study of solids, we also changed the name of our organizational unit to Department of Physical and Solid State Chemistry, and, as an independent worker, I took over reigns of heading it from the previous head, Dr Irena Kotula. At that time there were five adiunkts and three laboratory assistants (known as technical workers) in the Department. I began to teach fundamentals of crystal growth as an elective subject to senior students.

I set out to consolidate the scientific profile of the group by envisaging research work on some easily accessible interesting inorganic compounds, in addition to the organic aromatic compounds already being studied, and investigation of physical properties of solutions of the selected compounds from consideration of crystallization processes. The reason of inclusion of inorganic compounds for the investigations was that many of them could be grown from solutions prepared with water which is harmless, non-inflammable and cheap, but organic compounds could be grown from organic solvents which are frequently toxic, inflammable and relatively expansive. Bienek and Irena chose to continue their work with organic compounds, but Mieczysław Jakubczyk, Janusz Kliś and Halina Frej undertook the study of inorganic compounds. Since there was meagre scientific equipment for our investigations in those days, we had to depend on local home-made and, sometimes, obsolete or borrowed equipment. Bienek arranged my visit to one of the laboratories in the technical institution housed nearby, where we were promised to have the possibility of studying our crystals with a scanning electron microscope that they had. After the visit Bienek boasted of his different connections and acquaintances.

I could note a distinct difference in the ambiance here with that in my previous institution. Presence of colleagues in the previous place was usually confined to working hours and we remained engrossed in our teaching and research work most of the time. Exceptions were casual gathering to plan some collaborative research work, to discuss some results obtained by one of the colleagues or to drink together freshly prepared tea from brown-coloured packets of Madras-brand tea-leaves purchased by chance in some government grocery-store nearby in those days of socialism when there was not much to buy. We also enjoyed there to have lunch together in the dining-hall nearby. However, in the new institution there were regular celebrations of name-days of all employees of an organizational unit dur-

ing working hours, when the host-celebrator served his/her
visitors plenty of cakes and freshly-prepared sandwiches to
the teeth and some vodka to the throat. As well-cultured
persons, the visitors always came to attend the occasion
with some gift likely to be useful to the host later, but a
bottle of good vodka on this occasion was equally welcome.
There were also occasional days, such as days of inauguration of academic year, when larger groups of employees
from the faculty organised celebrations, on contribution
basis, in some spacious room or lecture hall in the evenings.
These celebrations continued for hours with abundant food
and drinks, accompanied by singing of popular songs, occasionally in chorus, and loud conversations on ill-defined
issues. Unpleasant situations also sometimes arose during
these celebrations when some of the boozed-up top functionaries of the Party affronted his/her colleague, by using
even indecent language, who did not agree with his opinion
or argument on the issue. These functionaries perhaps
manifested the leading role of the members of the Party
on such occasions. A large banner, with the slogan 'PZPR
Guiding Force of the Nation' fluttered in the spacious compound in front of the main building of the University of
Technology nearby.

In the College one could observe some of its technical maintenance personnel working after having a drink
or two during the working hours. Usually these persons
were cordial and well behaved, but they could be rude
when they felt that someone was violating their integrity.
Once a break down of water supply occurred in one of
the buildings in which a docent had his equipment. He
called the maintenance person to fix the break down. For
some reason the docent was not happy with the work of

this person and told him that he was talking to a docent. To this, in his shrill voice the visitor retorted: 'You are a docent of teaching. I am a docent of water pipes.' However, such incidents of arguments were rare, especially in the case of maintenance personnel who were in great demand.

In the initial period of my services we had our lunches in a dining hall situated on the other side of the road, but, after the collapse of socialism in 1989, we began to have our lunches in the newly started dining hall on the ground floor on the back side of the 'Red House', situated on Washington street in the city centre. This Red House had been Party's administrative building before and was called so because of its bright red colour, but its ownership rights were transferred to the College after the collapse of socialism. The Faculty of Humanities and Pedagogy, the Rectorate and the Central Administration of the College were also shifted to this Red House from Zawadzki Avanue. The College Pay-Office was set up close to the main gate, and hobnobing Wiesława Pyka, popularly called Wiesia, was the cashier. We collected our monthly salaries here. There were no modes of electronic transfer of salaries to banks in those days.

After joining my services in Częstochowa I felt the necessity of a textbook, written in the Polish language, for my teaching courses on elements of crystal growth to the fourth and fifth year students. In those days of socialism there were several books in this field in English, Russian and German languages. The problem with most of these books was that they not only covered somewhat narrow areas and were loaded with complicated mathematical outfit but they were not accessible in the main library of the College. Moreover, my students were neither good with mathematics nor with foreign languages. Therefore, I undertook the task of coordination of chapters on different topics, for a book on crystal growth in Polish, written by specialists in the country. For this purpose I approached prospective authors, by conventional post, explaining the aim of writing the book, with requests to write their chapters. Bienek's advice was indeed genuine in the preparation of the draft of my request to these prospective authors. Response to my requests varied from expressions of encouragement and all types of assistance in this endeavour to complete silence or doubts of my competence as a coordinator. The latter opinions reached me through two of the prospective authors of the group in the previous institute where I had been working on one-half position. They told that the boss of the group did not want them to participate in writing the chapter on growth of crystals from solutions. There was dead silence from the prospective authors of the Military Technical Academy, Warsaw.

When I met the boss of the group in the Institute during one of my working days there, I was surprised to know of the reason of his unwillingness. It was about my first book in English, with the affiliation of the Institute I had formally left. The book was published in The Netherlands. In those days it was a matter of prestige in the scientific circles to publish a book in the West by authors from the Socialist Countries. This poor boss felt cheated by not being a co-author in my book. When I asked for the reason, he argued that he contributed to its publication by making payments of typing costs of the manuscript. I was baffled by the argument, but retorted: 'I worked more than ten years on the manuscript.', and wanted to know the amount he paid for typing the manuscript.

In the entire period of service in the Institute the boss never talked of his authorship in my publications, and always boasted of papers published by colleagues from the group with my assistance. He did not even raise his eyebrows when he paid the typing costs of the manuscript of the book and I submitted it to North-Holland (renamed 'Elsevier' later) for publication in eighty-six. However, I did not understand why the issue of co-authorship arose after the appearance of printed version of the book. It occurred to me later that someone had made him understand that it was his folly not to be a co-author of the book published by his subordinate in the West. His adviser was certainly one of the bosses of groups in the country, who was a follower of the tradition of those days that every true boss deserves to be a co-author of every publication of his/her junior colleagues. Perhaps during his conversation with me the 'ex-boss' wanted to convey the message that he had imagined this type of chiefdom. But he knocked at a wrong door. Even the two colleagues, Barbara Wiktorowska and Telesfor Sokołowski, whom I approached, assured me of their willingness to contribute to the planned book in Polish, contrary to their Boss's intention.

I discovered that practically all authors kept their promise of writing their chapters within the specified time. Exception was one chapter on the theories and mechanism of crystal growth. After some time the authors from Warsaw, who I approached first, declined to submit their chapter up to the deadline due to their other commitments. They had published profoundly before in this area. Another group of authors, who I contacted afterwards, initially agreed, but they also expressed their inability to write this chapter. With two failed attempts to find appropriate authors and shrinking of time available to complete the manuscript up to the deadline, I decided to take up this formidable task myself somewhat hesitatingly because I never worked on theories of crystal growth. Fortunately, for the last several years I had been studying experimental aspects of problems related to fundamentals of crystal growth and had been using theoretical concepts of growth to interpret our experimental results. During these years I gathered a lot of reprints from the huge literature published on theories of crystal growth. This literature and our own experience were found to be adequate for writing our chapter.

Somewhere in March 1989 I planned to attend International Conference on Crystal Growth in Sendai, Japan. On my request the Organizers waived my Conference fees and promised me to cover expenses of my stay during the Conference. At that time I also accepted an offer of work, as a visiting scientist, for one year from September in the Institute of Materials of the Higher Council of Scientific Research (known by its Spanish acronym CSIC). That was the period of decline of the leading role of the Party, but banners reading 'PZPR Guiding Force of the Nation' could still be seen in the country. The Party Unit in the College was not certain whether the Party Officials were to approve my service trips. To the alleviation of many of us, obligatory approval of the Party for foreign visits was abandoned in May.

I submitted the final version of the manuscript of the book for publication to the Editorial Office of the College in June 1989. This was the time of transformation of political system in Poland. Socialism was on the verge of collapse, and the economy of the Country was in ruins. However, during the Conference in Sendai I came to know that a first non-communist government, lead by Tadeusz Mazowiecki, had been sworn in.

In the initial period of my services, Bienek sometimes accompanied me to my apartment and talked of functioning of our Department. During one of these strolls I felt that he was impressing upon how I should treat other members of the Department as their Head. He even bluntly told me once that he had imagined that Irena Kotula would continue to look after teaching affairs and I would look after scientific matters in the Department, but I had become the Head. Then I comprehended that he had dreamt of steering me from behind. Our days of amiability began to fade thereafter.

It was May or June 1989 when I came to know that Bienek had decided to split the Department and he had even received blessings from the College authorities. It was indeed a jolt for me. My regret was that Bienek did not inform me about his decision earlier, although I assisted him in the purchase of an optical microscope for him, with the money he managed to have from the College authorities, from Carl Zeiss company of East Germany. I arranged a meeting of the staff and asked them their opinion. Finally, Bienek, Irena and two of the technical workers decided to leave the Department, and formed a new group of Physical and Crystal Chemistry. We divided the rooms and the apparatus amicably. In those days it was rumoured that Bienek got an official coupon for purchase of a car from the disbanding party and that he bought a Fiat 126P car, popularly known as 'Maluch' (literally 'small'), on loan from PKO bank to establish a sheep farm.

After the vacations I departed to work in Barcelona for my yearly stay. Immediately on my arrival in Barcelona, with my host, Rafael Rodriguez-Clemente, we travelled to the historical city of El Escorial to participate in a scientific meeting on crystal growth. I was impressed by the atmosphere in that meeting. There arose the idea of organizing a crystal growth society in Poland. In this connection I contacted Anna Pajączkowska, who was working in the Institute of Physics, Polish Academy of Sciences. She appreciated the idea, but she was dissuaded from constituting an independent crystal growth society in the Country. The argument advanced in this connection was that a Crystal Growth Committee had been functioning for many years under the auspices of the Polish Academy of Sciences. However, the real hindrance was that some influential professors from known institutes, engaged in the activities of crystal growth and structure determination, were the office bearers of this Committee.

I spent my Christmas and Easter breaks in Częstochowa. During one of these breaks I came to know that Teresa Holi, one of the laboratory assistants in the Institute, was seriously ill and was a patient in the main hospital of the City. On the request of her husband, Andrzej Holi, I brought a medicine for her from Barcelona. In those days there was a problem with the availability of medicines in Poland. However, after some time she expired. It was a big blow to Andrzej because he was left with two tiny tots, a son and a daughter, to raise without Teresa. Andrzej was of the opinion that negligence of the doctors of the hospital was the reason of her wife's death. Many of us could not believe that this gentle and sober woman was no more with us. The Holis enjoyed serving us home-fermented wine on their name-days celebrated in the Institute. Once Teresa promised to serve me the new wine they were brewing. Alas, she could not keep the promise.

In Barcelona, we finalised the manuscript of a book on surfaces of crystalline and non-crystalline solids for a Swiss publisher. After the stay there at the end of August, I took my return flight to Warsaw with a heavy baggage containing diskettes of computer-written text of the manuscript and plenty of reprints of papers and books for my future use. Marta, my wife, who had stayed with me in Barcelona during her vacations, accompanied me during this return flight. I remember that I paid a lot of pesetas for the excess baggage of this flight.

On my return to Częstochowa I saw the printed version of the book on crystal growth under the imprint of WSP, Częstochowa. I came to know that the book was printed in Warsaw. I was somewhat disappointed by the poor quality of paper used for the printing, but remained quiet in view of scarcity of practically everything and enormous inflation in the Country at that time.

A new law of Ministry of Higher Education, changing names of academic positions, came into force from the new academic year commencing from September 1990. The positions of docents were transformed to time-specific extraordinary professors, and the previous posts of extraordinary and ordinary professors were transformed to the posts of permanent extraordinary and ordinary professors, with the prerequisite of a professor's title conferred by the President of Poland. Therefore, obeying the spirit of this new law, Rector Polanowski was obliged to appoint all teachers afresh on new posts. Since he was a docent, he first took the appointment of an extraordinary professor from one of his subordinate professors and then he appointed all docents in the College to the posts of extraordinary professors. Thus, I became an extraordinary professor of the College. The Rector also assigned to me an official apartment to live on ulica Księżycowa ((in English 'Lunar street') nearby. In the elections to the College administration I was elected to the Senate as its senator and Józef Świątek was elected as the Rector.

In the beginning of the academic year Ewa Mielniczek joined the Department as an assistant. She had completed her diploma work for her master's degree in our Department under the supervision of Janusz Kliś. We also received a grant from the Ministry of Higher Education to purchase some scientific instruments for our research work. With this grant we purchased, among others, an optical microscope, a viscometer and a couple of thermostats.

Somewhere at the end of December 1990, I began to attend classes of car driving. In the very first attempt I cleared both written and practical driving tests. While I was driving the test-car in the city from Jasna Góra monastery, the examiner, called Kowalczyk, made attempts to direct me to commit mistakes, but he was pleased to note that I was very cautious with the driving rules and signs and my capability. Some days later I collected my driving license from the City Council.

My research work until now had been on the border of physical chemistry and solid state physics but, starting from my master's degree, I received my later degrees in physics. Therefore, I was in a dilemma whether to continue my work here in Częstochowa in the Institute of Chemistry or to shift to some other institution where I could contribute to physics and have an opportunity of being awarded a title of professor of physical sciences. Attitude of Józef Świątek, who had been the Director of the Institute of Physics over years, to my proposal of supervising diploma work of students from his Institute was also unfriendly. Marta had resigned from her previous job and had decided to shift to Lublin to look after her ageing parents. Therefore, I had wavering ideas of continuing my job in Częstochowa after my return from Barcelona.

Inspired by the activities of Spanish colleagues I began to organize the inaugural meeting of the Polish Society for Crystal Growth (in Polish 'Polskie Towarzystwo Wzrostu Kryształów') in Częstochowa in the second half of May 1991 and to contact its possible participants. I selected this period to avoid competition with triennial International Conferences on Crystal Growth organised in June or July in different continents and other biennial national meetings organized usually in September and October. In view of my uncertainty of continuing work here in the future I convinced Professor Stanisław Hodorowicz of Jagiellonian University in Cracow to have the official seat of the Society in Cracow.

Local chapters of the national Chemical and Physical Societies operative in Częstochowa occasionally organized lectures on specific topics of interest by invited speakers. Professor Marian Herman was one of these invited speakers. He gave a nice talk on epitaxy in the College. He had been working in the Institute of Physics of the Academy. He began his journey from Waraw to Częstochowa, a distance of some three-hundred kilometers, early in the morning at about 7 o'clock, by his 'Maluch', the small Fiat 126P car, and after the lecture he returned to Warsaw on the same day. His modesty and cordiality again impressed me enormously. He earlier wrote two chapters for the book of crystal growth and assisted me in finding authors to write some other chapters. Those were the days when some of the colleagues of the College, who had been studying superconducting properties of crystalline solids, suggested to me to grow materials for them. I declined the suggestion and argued that I was a boss in my field but I would become nobody in the field of superconducting materials because I would the last author in the list of authors of papers on the materials grown for them. In those days our colleague, Janusz Kliś, started skipping his teaching responsibilities due to his addiction to vodka. I visited his house and made attempts to assist him. I regretted that he could not keep his job despite my sincere efforts.

I submitted the manuscript of the book on surfaces in the form of camera-ready copy for the Swiss publisher in early 1991. Some months later this book was published. I received some copies of the book from the Publisher for my personal use and two thousand German marks as its royalty. Roughly then I received an offer of working as a professor in the Department of Physics, Lublin University of Technology (in Polish 'Politechnika Lubelska'). I accepted the offer and agreed to join the new position in Lublin from the coming academic year.

As an organizer of the meeting of the Society for Crystal Growth, I had two main problems with its organization. First, I had to invite some eminent scientist from the Country to deliver the first lecture, which I decided to call 'Czochralski Lecture' to commemorate the outstanding contribution of Jan Czochralski to crystal growth from melts by a method known by his name. He was a professor in Politechnika Warszawska (in English: Warsaw University of Technology), before the Second World War, and was later condemned by the Communist Rule in Poland for his 'supposed' collaboration with the Nazis. Second, for the functioning of the Society we were to vote its constitution during the meeting.

I found Professor Julian Auleytner from the Institute of Physics, Polish Academy of Sciences, Warsaw, the best choice for the Czochralski Lecture. He was an authority in the field of x-ray diffraction techniques and was a modest person. He also happened to be a 'dark' reviewer chosen by the Central Qualification Commission for the evaluation of my scientific output for the award of a habilitation degree. I had known before the names of three referees for the evaluation of my scientific output, but I remained in the 'dark' until Professor Auleytner himself disclosed to me later that he was a referee appointed by the Central Qualification Commission.

After a perusal of constitutions of a couple of national societies, I decided to prepare a draft of the constitution of our crystal growth society following the constitution of the Polish Physical Society, with suitable modifications regarding the structure of its governing body. My observations of elections to the governing bodies of different societies affirmed my belief that their constitutions were not only adverse to the victory of young and promising candidates as presidents for a tenure during elections of officials of the societies by its members in the general assemblies but discouraged candidature of such candidates. The reason was that these young candidates worked in groups and institutions with the seniors at the helm, and these seniors expected to be officials of the societies. Since the tenure of a governing body started after the elections, these seniors were the natural candidates over years, and there was no instrument that prevented them from being elected as presidents until their retirement from services. To avoid situations which discouraged elections of young members for the office of president of our newly constituted Society of Crystal Growth, we envisaged provisions in the Constitution of three time-bound tenures of its President as President-Elect, President and Past-President.

The two-day inaugural meeting of the planned Society was held in Częstochowa, with invited lectures and posters by its participants, and acceptance of its Constitution. Professor Auleytner delivered the Czochralski Lecture, and Professor Anna Pajączkowska was elected its first President and Professor Stanisław Hodorowicz its President-Elect. Participation in the meeting was modest. There were less than twenty participants in all, including two technical assistants, Irena Wekiera and Andrzej Holi, who assisted in its organization. Unfortunately, Bienek's group, and crystal growers from my previous Institute in Łódź and Military Technical Academy in Warsaw boycotted it. The Society was finally registered in a Court in Cracow, with its seat in Jagiellonian University, in 1992 when I was working in Lublin.

I was overjoyed to see that even researchers from the groups of institutions, who remained absent previously, actively participated in the next meeting of the Society held in Cracow, and Professor Marian Herman was elected its President-Elect.

March 2023

5

IN TURKEY

IN THE DAYS OF MY EARLY CHILDHOOD I heard, with my
ears wide open, various narrations of village life before the
country's partition. Some of these narrations were witty,
others had tinge of sadness and guilt, but there were some
miscellaneous ones with specific labels for certain sections
of the Society.

A thánedár came to our village on an official enquiry of
some theft. To assist the thánedár the villagers assembled
under the shadows of trees of village takiyá. Problem arose
of serving food and water to him because he was a Muslim.
Following the customs of those days, he was willing to
have food cooked only in a Muslim family. Fortunately, a
Muslim family lived in the village, and all were relieved
of the problem. Therefore, willingly or unwillingly the
head of the family, Kamaroodeen, took the responsibility
of feeding the thánedár.

At the outset of his undertaking Kamaroodeen brought
a bowl of curd. After seeing the solid curd in Kamaroodeen's hands, the thánedár instructed him in Punjábi to add
some water to the curd and "rirhak" the mass. The verb
"rirhak" means "stir" in Punjábi but is equivalent of the
verb "moo" in the village dialect, which poor Kamaroodeen
knew. This simple peasant understood that this mooing
is perhaps some sort of ceremony before drinking curd.
Equipped with thánedár's command Kamaroodeen timidly
went some yards away from the meeting place and, behind
a wall, made loud sounds of mooing a couple of times and

131

returned to the meeting place. All laughed. Then someone from the village instructed Kamaroodeen what he was to do precisely. Those were the days when illiterate inhabitants of our village were poorly versed with the Punjábi language unlike today when everyone speaks both Punjábi and Hindi in the entire Punjáb and the spoken dialect of old days of our area has become more comprehensive for others due to frequent mutual contacts and free use of many words from other languages.

Religion-based partition of the country in 1947 disrupted the entire life of the society and created mistrust among believers of different religions. This resulted in the migration of caravans of Hindu and Sikh population living in the areas of the newly carved Pákistán to the remaining part of India and of Muslim population living in the regions of carved-out India to Pákistán. Migration of people of one faith in caravans assured better security during their mobility through villages and towns with population of other faith. Protection of the population of these villages and towns was organized in such a way that groups of women, children and elder males were formed at some space and young males guarded all entrances to them from attacks by outsiders.

There were no untoward incidences of attacks in our village. In general, the guards outside the village did not come across migrating caravans. Exception was a stray instance of a Muslim weaver who had to pass past our village to go ahead to West Pákistán. Some young guards took notice of him and killed. But there were many people in the village who felt sorry for this incidence later.

I frequently heard in those days branding Muslims as "Turks." I never understood why they were called so. I learned that they followed the same social structure as Hindus and Sikhs and differed from them only by religion. I was certain that they did not come from Turkey. I came to know about this country in history classes in the school. Some years later I came to know of "young Turks" functioning in the Congress Party. But I did not understand why they were called "Turks." They were Indian citizens, most of them followers of Hinduism, and represented different constituencies of the country in the Parliament as its elected members. Perhaps they were branded so because they expressed their opinions on current issues in their Party loudly and frankly like a group of turkeys gobbling in the courtyard of their master.

After shifting to Poland in the nineteen eighty I concentrated on establishing myself as an academic teacher in the initial period and for many years I regularly spent my summer holidays mainly in the hilly area of south of Poland. The reason was that I liked the ambience of the area and the hospitality of our hosts. In those days visas were required by Polish passport holders to travel to the other so-called western countries to participate in international scientific events organized there. My Indian passport was useful in these participations because it was easy to obtain a visa on this passport without standing in long queues in the embassies of western countries for this purpose. This passport was of course a hindrance in travelling to the former Soviet-bloc countries, but fortunately not many important events were organized there. However, after political transformations in Poland things began to change. The number of western countries waiving visa requirement for Polish nationals steadily increased, but visa requirements remained unmoved on my Indian passport.

Judging pros and cons of retaining Indian nationality, I released it just before the end of the twentieth century and became a Polish national.

In mid nineties former Soviet-bloc countries witnessed a spurt of tourist companies specialized in organizing trips to spend holidays in countries of stable weather. In those days among the popular tourist destinations were Turkey, Egypt, Morroco and Croatia. One of my compatriots, Satya Kanwal, living in Łódź regularly availed of the services of these tourist companies and later used to tell us experiences of his family spending holidays in these countries. Fascinated by these and other narrations, in 2003 I also decided to spend my holidays with Marta on the beaches of the resort city of Alanya in the Mediterranean region of Turkey and purchased a two-week package from one of the tourist companies operating in Lublin. Alanya lies in the slopes of Taurus Mountain and is situated in the Antalya Province.

Following the programme we were transported to the Chopin Airport in Warsaw by luxury buses, and from there we flew to Antalya Airport by a chartered plane. After passport control at the Antalya Airport we were received by our resident guide, who directed us to buses waiting for us to carry to Alanya. We reached our hotel in Alanya in the hot hours of the afternoon. During this journey I saw small tea-stalls on road sides in a manner similar to what I had known before while travelling in India in summer. Immediately after our registration at the hotel reception we had our first so-called Swiss-style lunch-cum-dinner in the restaurant of the hotel. Content with relishing the food items laid on the table in the restaurant hall, we set out to know our surrounding area.

Next day after taking a heavy breakfast we went to explore our experiments with relaxing on the beach near the hotel. First dip in the warm water of the sea was exceptionally pleasant, but the increasing air temperature with the rise of the Sun drove us back to the hotel after some time to have some soft drinks. For the first time I had crimson-coloured tea served in small dumbbell-shaped glasses. I noticed later that these glasses were omnipresent in Turkey.

Our zest of spending morning and evening hours on the beach slowly faded away and we began to use this time in going on excursions organized, at additional costs to forest areas in the mountain, by our resident guide and in visiting the city market. We purchased two excursions. The first was a one-day safari on a jeep to the mountains in the nearby areas and the second was a two-day excursion to the Cappadocia region.

During the first excursion we had the opportunity of seeing some deer freely walking in the woods and enjoyed lunch in an open-air restaurant with tables and chairs arranged on a bridge-like structure of wooden desks on a narrow rivulet of fresh water flowing under the shades of trees. During the second excursion we visited a porcelain factory and a carpet factory and enjoyed the unique landscape of pillars, cone-like structures, valleys, and caves of the Cappadocia region developed over time by erosion of the relatively soft volcanic rock. The Cappadocia region is situated to the north of the Taurus Mountains in the centre of Turkey. We were fascinated by the landscape of this region. We gathered an impression that large complexes of man-made caves and underground tunnels built or expanded from existing structures probably served as hiding places for early Christians and that structures of caves and passages through adjoining caves ensured natural ventilation between them as well as free movement of the inhabitants. Rock-cut churches and chapels, some with beautiful frescoes inside, scattered throughout the countryside are symbols of turbulent periods in the history of the region.

We had exhilarating experience with purchasing petty articles in the city market. We observed that the prices of articles given by the shop owners were usually double the prices a client could bargain ultimately and after the deal the shopkeeper ordered Turkish-style tea to be taken together with the client in dumb-bell-shaped glasses, from the nearest tea-stall, as a token of success of the transaction. I enjoyed this type of tea of success while purchasing a couple of cotton shirts from a shop whose middle-aged owner knew Turkish only, but the successful deal of my shirts was possible with the services of one of the shopkeeper's neighbours who served as a translator between us. These shopkeepers were highly pleased to know that I hailed from India. I still remember the smiling face of the shopkeeper with whom I had tea. With his dyed hair he could have easily passed as one of the shopkeepers in Punjáb.

The European Union (EU) has several programmes which enable EU academic institutions such as universities to establish scientific and teaching collaboration with non-EU institutions. One of these programmes is Erasmus, which enables mobility of students as well as academic staff of universities of different countries. In the framework of this programme for example, students of Polish universities can complete one or two semesters of their studies in foreign universities, and conversely, students from foreign universities complete their semesters in Polish universities. Under this programme I had the opportunity of teaching small groups of students from Turkey, Italy and Morroco for two semesters. There is also a programme of mobility of academic teachers, which enables academic teachers of the university of one country to give lectures on a mutually-agreed topic in the university of another country. Usually these trips of teachers are of short durations.

For many years I thought that short trips of academic staff require big efforts but the final gain is small. First of all, the prospective visitor has to find a host in the country of paying a visit, then, on specific topics agreed with the host, he/she has to prepare appropriate lectures to be delivered in the host university, and finally he/she has to arrange a substitution for the teaching schedule during his/her absence in the parent university. However, after many years I decided to avail myself of the Erasmus Programme and visit Mustafa Kemal University (Mustafa Kemal Universitesi; MKU) located in Antokya in Hatay Province in Turkey.

I found that Dr Osmán Sáhin of the Department of Physics (Fizik Bülümü) in the Faculty of Pure Sciences and Arts (Fen Edebiyat Fakültesi) in MKU had been studying mechanical properties of alloys. I had been working in this area since the days of my doctoral studies. Therefore, I contacted him whether he would like to be my host there. Thanks to e-mail services, I received his quick response in the affirmative. Then we agreed mutually that I would visit MKU for six days in May 2013 and give three lectures on the following topics: (1) microhardness measurements on crystalline and noncrystalline solids, (2) crystal growth as a scientific discipline, and (3) on our scientific output.

Mustafa Kemal University is located in the city of Antakya. Following suggestions from Dr Sáhin I planned my trip from Warsaw to Antakya by plane with a transfer of flight at Istanbul Airport. After check-in at Chopin Airport in Warsaw I purchased a couple of chocolate boxes in one of the tax-free shops as a present for my host. I took my flight to Istanbul by Turkish Airlines, where I landed early in the afternoon. Since there was only one flight to Antakya late in the evening, I had plenty of time to walk around in the interior of the airport. Finally, we boarded our plane to Antakya. In the plane I could see some of my co-passengers in typical Arabian-style dress. After about two hours our plane landed at the Antakya Airport, where just at the exit gate Dr Sáhin and one young man from the Foreign Collaboration Section of the University received me with a bouquet of flowers. Then they guided me to a car belonging to the University, which took us to the University Guest House. It was quite hot outside and the air-conditioner in the apartment took some time to attain the desired temperature. I solved the problem of seeing the flowers withering in the apartment by handing over the bouquet to Dr Sáhin with a request to pass it on to his wife. Before his departure, he informed me that he would come to pick me up in the morning to his Department of Physics.

Early in the morning I was somewhat disturbed from sleep by calls of morning prayers on loudspeaker from the nearby mosque, but I continued to idle away despite the noisy calls for prayers until the breakfast in the Guest House restaurant and Dr Osmán Sáhin's arrival to take me to the university in an official car. We reached the Department of Physics where Osmán introduced me to the Head of the Department and its other members. There I was given a warm welcome with all of us taking traditional tea in dumbbell-shaped glasses.

Mustefa Kemal University is relatively recent of modern architecture. It was founded in 1992 and has general profile of education in diverse fields such as engineering, medicine, veterinary, fishery, natural sciences, humanities and education. The hosts made all efforts to show me different faculties, laboratories, and university library. I did not observe any religious symbol in the University, but there were portraits of Mustefa Kemal Atatürk, founder of the present Turkey, hanging on the walls adjoining the dais in lecture halls and seminar rooms. In view of the fact that practically the entire Turkish society is follower of Islam, the university staff is also mainly adherent of Islam. Academic teachers frequently worship in their offices behind closed doors on special mats or carpets during intervals between lessons. Once when I was in his office discussing something, Osmán asked me to excuse him for interrupting our conversation because he had to worship. Then he spread a mat hidden behind the door of his office and began to worship.

Hatay region is known for its ancient history. The first reference to Antikya appears in the Bible as Antiochia. It is believed that St Peter spent the early years of his preaching here. The Church of St Peter is the reminiscent of this site. Hatay Archaeology Museum is another place of historical importance concerning evolution of Christianity in this region. Then there is Habib-i-Najjar Mosque of very recent past. Therefore, my hosts made maximum efforts to show me different sites of historical importance. Apart from the above sites, my host Osmán entrusted one of his friends and his family to organize a trip to visit old historical remnants close to the Syrian border. We visited an Armenian Monastery on our way to the border with Syria.

During our journey I was fascinated to see women baking large bread on an iron plate placed on a hearth heated by burning dry wood periodically in it and a dark-complexioned hefty man, with curly moustache, nearby baking loaves in a vertical earthen oven, called "tandeer" in Turkey, red-heated before baking by burning dry tree branches. Except for some modification in the dimensions of the hearth and the oven, I found the art of baking bread in these two ways there similar to that used in Punjáb. We had our lunch in an open-air restaurant under the shade of an old banyan tree.

One evening Osmán invited me to his house to have supper with his family. He also invited one of his colleagues. We were seated on a carpet spread on the floor of the entire drawing room. I handed over the chocolate boxes to Osmán's wife. Though Osmán's wife is a house-wife, we could communicate in English, but she and Osmán mostly remained busy with the preparation of food. Osmán's two young sons surrounded me on the carpet from either side and were curious to know different things from me by asking in Turkish only. Osmán's friend served as a translator and solved the problem of my communication with the boys in replies to their enquiries. After the translation of each of my replies, I frequently asked the boys by quipping the Turkish word "tamám." The boys expressed their joy to hear this word from me and loudly commented that

I spoke Turkish. I had learnt the word "tamám" during conversations in the University and represented "okay" in Turkish instead of "all" in Hindi.

Next day Osmán returned me one of the chocolate boxes and informed that there was alcohol in the chocolate pieces and that he had to return them because Islam did not permit them to consume products containing alcohol. I indeed discovered that there was alcohol in the chocolate pieces. I regretted my mistake because I did not check when I purchased them in the Warsaw Airport.

During one of our conversations Osmán explained to me about his research activities. He told that he had been following my publications since the early days of his research work. It was indeed a matter of pride for me to know this. Then I understood the significance of the bouquet of flowers from him at the Antakya Airport on my arrival there.

A day before my departure some students came to present me a copy of the original Arabic version of the holy Korán with its English translation and a book on the legends of Habib-i-Najjar Mosque in English. That day evening Osmán took me to the city bazaar, where he did some purchases for his house in shops whose owners appeared to be known to him since long. However, he surprised me by handing me over a bag containing various spices and bottles of Turkish-origin olive oil to carry to Lublin.

After the visit I simply turned over the pages of the Korán and made no serious attempt to go through it because I had studied its Hindi translation before. However, since I knew nothing about Habib-i-Najjar, I was curious to know the contents of the book on Habib-i-Najjar Mosque.

Although the authors of the book tried to trace the history of Habib-i-Najjar to the early days of Islam, the arguments given there appeared to me to be far-fetched and suggested that they were legends rather authentic history.

Before the outbreak of Coronavirus epidemic in 2019 our University has been organizing every year various sight-seeing tours of Europe for its staff and their family members. After a hesitance for some years, we began to take part in these tours. The main advantage of these organized tours is that most of its participants are known to each other and sightseeing and travelling by a hired tourist bus is during daytime with appropriate breaks to stretch legs by swaggering outside the luxury bus. The organized schedule of the tours enables the participants to have breakfast and lunch at appropriate time and to sleep reasonably well at night. The only disadvantage is that some unforeseen incident can happen somewhere. One of these tours in which we participated was a ten-day guided tour of Turkey in August/September 2013.

On the day of our departure we gathered in front of the building of our university mess, where we boarded a tourist bus before dawn to depart to Serbia via Slovakia and Hungary. After a stay for the night in a hotel close to Belgrad, we travelled to Bulgaria and then, after crossing the Turkish border at Edirne, we reached Istanbul practically before midnight due to traffic jams on the way. In Istanbul we spent two hectic days visiting Hagia Sophia Museum, Blue Mosque and Sultan's Palace, among others. From there we visited limy terraces of Pamukkale and ancient city of Hierapolis, archaeological monuments in Efes, and Meryemana Sanctuary. Then we spent two days to relax on the beaches of Didim. After the rest in Didim we visited, among others, ancient ruins of Troy and replica of Troy's horse. Finally, after spending a night in Gelibolu in Turkey we departed to return to Lublin. On our way we had the opportunity of spending our Turkish liras in buying petty articles and presents in some markets. In one of these markets I was tempted to buy a half-kilogram packet of Brooke Bond tea for consumption at home. Thereafter once again we had a night stay on the outskirts of Belgrad where we first had late supper in the evening on our arrival and early breakfast in the morning before our departure to Lublin.

I took photographs of practically all important sites that we visited during the trip with the sole purpose of registering changes in the history of our civilization. For example, Hagia Sophia (literally: Holy Wisdom) in Istanbul was built according to Greek designers as the Christian cathedral of Constantinople for the Byzantine Empire in the sixth century. It was used as an Eastern Orthodox church until the conquest of Constantinople by the Ottoman Empire in the fifteenth century, when it was converted to a mosque and Islamic architectural additions, including four minarets, replaced Christian iconography, such as the mosaic depictions of Jesus, Mary, Christian saints and angels. Hagia Sophia served as a mosque until 1935, when it became a museum under the secular Republic of Turkey. However, in 2020 the Turkish State once again classified the site as a mosque.

Pamukkale-Hierapolis complex is located in the southwestern Turkey. Pamukkale, meaning "cotton castle" in Turkish, is an area where hot limestone-rich water flows down slowly the mountainside and collects into pools and cascades into travertine terraces, forming an unusual landscape of pools and terraces. The Turkish name refers to the surface of the shimmering, snow-white limestone, shaped over millennia by calcite-rich springs.

The area of old Hierapolis (Holy City) comprises ruins of temples, churches, amphitheaters and necropolis of the Byzantine and Roman periods. Hierapolis as well as Efes area remained important centres for Christianity and are remnants of rich and diverse architectural skills of the period of our civilization.

In recent years the Turkish Government has been making all efforts to popularize the name of the country as Türkiye instead of the popularly known name Turkey. The purpose of these efforts is to delink the name of the country from the bird Turkey. Alas, unaware of controversy, this bird has become one of its sides but has no influence on the acceptance or approval of the name of the country in the World community.

I remember my visits to Turkey, sorry Türkiye, for acquiring knowledge of turbulence in history from the ruins of amphitheatres, buildings, verses from Koran added to the Greek text in the Sophia Church, and efforts of Atatürk in bringing the Turkish society closer to the West by replacing the old Arabic alphabet by the Latin alphabet and introducing administrative reforms. Above all, I remember these visits for the tea in dumbbell-shaped glasses during my visits and the packet of tea that I enjoyed for several months much later after its purchase.

August 2022

6

DAMNED FAMILY

DURING THE SECOND HALF of the nineteenth century colonial Britishers sold chunks of empty land in the old Ferozepur district to individuals for organization of permanent settlements engaged in developing farming in the area. With the incentive of owners of these carved out area of the land, initial settlers built their indigenous houses from locally available raw materials haphazardly in the proximity of an artificial or natural pond to collect drinking water during rainy season for the entire year. With time as more houses were built the settlement grew with several irregular, curved streets frequently spanning from some central free compound surrounded by the houses built first.

Some ten miles away to the north of the city of Abohar there is village called Chuhriwálá Dhanna. This village is not different from most of the villages founded in the second half of the nineteenth century. During the sixties of the last century the village had an empty central compound with several irregular streets going out from it and a long practically straight street ran to the north from this compound. Nearly in the centre of this compound stood a huge banyan tree surrounded by a wide chowkee which the village men-folk frequently used to spend long summer noons when they played cards excitedly or had nap on the chárpayees they had brought from their homes.

After the war of 1965, my younger sister Dropadi was married off in the above village. Her father-in-law's house lay somewhat on the outer part of the village on a street zigzagging to the south-west from the central compound. Apart from the demise of her father-in-law, during the last five decades her family has undergone enormous changes due to setting up of families by her husband's brothers, division of the family property, construction of a separate house by the family of her husband's younger brother and migration of the elder brother to Delhi. During the last two decades, her daughter and two sons have set up their own families, but her family still lives with her husband and one of her sons in the old family house, which has taken new form with the changing days, and looks after their piece of agricultural land.

Some years after my sister's marriage, my niece Santro was also married off in this village. Her husband, Manphool, and his school-going younger brother, Om, were the only children in the family, who lived with their parents in a house, situated not far off from the central compound of the village, on the western row of houses on the straight street stretching to the north. The family lived from earnings of traditional summer and winter crops grown in some twenty acres of land which her father-in-law inherited from his parents. Her mother-in-law was a typical housewife looking after the needs of the family members. As is the order set by the Almighty, her in-laws left for heavenly abode after sometime and Manphool took the responsibility of running the family. As the time passed, Om set up his own family and Santro's son, Jagdish, and daughter, Saritá, began to have their school education.

Being the elder of the two brothers, Manphool looked after the farming of the inherited agricultural land in the village for some years, but later he decided to expand the family resources by starting some new business apart from seasonal harvests from the fields. It occurred to the brothers to purchase more agricultural fields elsewhere from the sale of the inherited fields in the village and to enter into the business of manufacturing and marketing accumulators of jeeps and tractors. To reach their goal, they purchased a piece of agricultural land in Hastinápur, a historical place in western Uttar Pradesh, about 23 miles from Meerut and 60 miles north-east of Delhi, much more than they had in the village, from the money they obtained by selling their ancestral fields. For some time the brothers cultivated themselves the piece of land in Hastinápur, where they found enormous support from their neighbours, a Sikh family, who had settled there some years ago. During this period of residence in Hastinápur, one of the two brothers of this family became Santro's brother, known as dharam bhái, with a vow of mutual trust and sincerity. However, Satro's family did not live there for long. Instead, they leased the cultivation of their fields to their 'neighbours' on yearly basis and shifted to settle in the well-prospering city of Hanumángarh to set up business of accumulators. Hanumángarh is some 40 miles south of Abohar and the two cities are well connected by an asphalted road. It was here that Manphool split the joint property with his brother. Both Jagdish and Saritá also got married later. Jagdish remained with his parents, but Saritá began to live with her husband's family in Hanumángarh Junction.

Manphool established his own showroom for sale of accumulators in Hanumángarh Junction and his son, Jagdish, set up a factory, on the outskirts of the city, for the production of accumulators. With time the business with accumulators prospered well, and the family sold their agricultural fields in Hastinápur and invested the so-received money in the factory. Since the business rolled unusually well, Manphool's family began to build a big house. However, the family faced heavy losses in the business due to a wrong bank loan when their house was still under construction. Therefore, to save the morose financial situation of the family, they sold the partially-built house and shifted to a smaller house not far off from the house of Saritá's in-laws. And the family set out to lead a normal and peaceful life in the new house.

Manphool became a staunch disciple of Rádhá Soami Satsang of Beás and even began to participate in its congregations. He was strongly influenced by the teachings of the Satsang and frequently spoke about these teachings, but I never saw Santro performing any religious ceremonies and talking about religious morality. Whenever we met, she remembered funny events of her childhood to make us laugh and gave me lessons on cooking karhee which I always relished.

The first wave of Corona virus disease 2019 (popularly known as Covid-19), caused by infection of SARS-CoV-2 virus, appeared in India in the beginning of March 2021 and the first signs of its presence were noted in participants of religious and social festivities. Since people from different places participate in these religious and social festivities, they were ideal for the rapid spread of this fatal virus in different parts of the Country. I remember that some people from villages of Fazilka area participated in Ardh Kumbh Mela, and, after their return home from the Mela, most of them were victims of this virus. Unfortunately, it was also the period of marriages when relatives and friends from different places gathered in marriage celebrations. After the marriages, practically all of their participants were sufferers of this virus. Although there was a vigorous vaccination drive against the spread of Covid-19 by the Government, there were many who did not believe that something invisible like the Covid-19 virus could lead to fatal consequences. Hearsay miracles of cure of Covid-virus patients by known herbs and some frequently-used medicines and anti-vaccination lobby in the electronic media, which doubted the very existence of this virus, added to the tales of woes of the common man.

Santro and her husband, Manphool, attended a marriage ceremony in Srigangánagar, and after the marriage returned home happily. The vaccination drive against Covid was in full swing then, but this couple ignored it entirely. Sometime later Manphool began to have symptoms of persistent cough and fever due to Covid-19, and needed medical care. Judging the situation at home and hearing news of increasing number of Covid patients every day in those day, Santro took the first anti-Covid vaccination.

Despite medical treatment by doctors available in the city, Manphool did not recover from Covid and after some days succumbed to it. With all precautions, his body was given due last cremation rites. Some days later Santro and her son, Jagdish, also began to show symptoms of Covid. Fortunately, Jagdish recovered after taking medicament under the guidance of doctors, but Santro's condition deteriorated with time and she began to have severe respiratory problems. Doctors in the city, who had been treating her, advised her attendants to take her to some better-equipped hospital in Srigangánager, where she could be assured of continuous inhaling of oxygen.

Enquiries in prospective hospitals in Srigangánager revealed that they were experiencing shortage of oxygen for their patients and did not admit new Covid patients for treatment. Situation in the government hospital in Bathindá was not different. However, it turned out that, in Bathindá, a multi-speciality private hospital, called Jiviya, agreed to admit Santro. Therefore, Santro was taken to this hospital in Bathindá from Hanumángarh, by a special transport, by four of her family members at the end of April. She remained in this hospital, for complete ten days, with these family members to attend upon her in different shifts. On the tenth day, Santro expired in the hospital, but the hospital issued a certificate that she was relieved from it after her treatment. In connection with Santro's treatment in the private hospital, the family lodged a complaint with the Deputy Commissioner, Bathindá, but the matter was hushed up by various officials at different levels.

There were three aspects of Santro's treatment in the above private hospital in Bathindá. First, despite claims by the hospital-in-charge that the patient was recovering, Santro expired. Second, from the very first day this hospital-in-charge charged Rs 25,000 per day in cash (i.e. Rs 250,000, in total) for her treatment in the hospital without issuing a receipt of the received money. Everyday one of the members of Santro's family attending on her had to go to some ATM machine in the area to collect the amount in cash for payment to the hospital-in-charge. Third, all of her four family members were in constant contact with Covid-infected Santro in the hospital. Some of them developed cough there and, after her death, fearing that they might be infected by the Corona virus, all of them went into self-isolation in their houses and swallowed pills for weeks. Fortunately, they showed negative tests later and became active again in their work thereafter.

After the demise of his parents, Jagdish was left in the family by his wife and two minor, school-going, daughters. Now it was Jagdish's responsibility to look after the family and to run the family business. The worst thing was to reconstruct business transactions of sales of accumulators by the father. Finally, he fixed up his financial situation and, despite uncertain return of some of the payments by buyers of the accumulators from the showroom, began to build up his business for a normal future. However, whether it was a consequence of after-effects of Covid-19 or constitution of his body itself, he grew fatter with time.

During the second half of December 2022, Jagdish developed some pain in the stomach. Since this pain persisted for some time, he was admitted in a hospital in Hisár where it was discovered that his kidneys had been infected. Despite best efforts of the doctors attending upon Jagdish, on the fifth day he expired in the hospital due to kidney failure. Then his body was brought back to Hanumángarh for cremation by his nearest members of the family. Some days after Jagdish's cremation, these members discovered that the house was mortgaged for a sum of some twelve lakhs of rupees. Therefore, the nearest members of the family decided to pay off this mortgage to support the three unfortunate women left behind in the house. The relatives and friends of this family were so engulfed in their misfortune and sorrow that it did not occur to any of them to celebrate the nearest Holi festival.

March 2023

7

AFTER FIFTY-FOUR YEARS OF INDEPENDENCE

THE MOTIVATION FOR WRITING THIS ESSAY comes from a thought-provoking contribution in the "Opinions" section of The Tribune, under the title "After Thirty Years", by Prof. Ihasar. In his contribution the author describes his views on Pákistán-Bangládesh relations after thirty years of secession from the post-partition Pákistán. In general, he is right in his analysis of the failure of the co-existence of East and West Pákistán. He correctly concludes that the then West Pákistán, despite being in minority, wanted to dominate the majority Eastern part economically and politically. In his opinion, now it is not possible for Pákistán and Bangládesh to exist together as one state but they can have good relations in view of the common existence of the two countries as a state for 25 years and the common religion.

I believe that any two neighbours, whether they are human-beings or states, should have good relations. However, a quick look at the relations between different countries of the World shows that in order to have good relations between two neighbouring or far-off countries there is no need to have a common past. Examples at hand are most of the European countries, Germany and France included, and the relations between USA and UK and between USA and Canada. Common religion is also not a binding force forging good relations. There are numerous examples, some

153

of them are: Pákistán and Bangládesh, Czech and Slovak Republics, Peoples' Republic of China and Taiwan, and South and North Koreas. In all these cases the cause of discord is simply the inclination of a few people to dominate the other by every possible means. The possible means are based on three ideologies: political, religious and economical. All these people have one aim: to rule others.

Political and religious ideologies are cultivated by the so-called ideologists and propagated by their followers or subordinates. Nazism, Communism and Tálibán-type movements fall in this category. Unfortunately, both ideologists and propagators never make attempts to foresee the future of the society or country due to lack of appropriate social and educational background and start living in their own castles erected on unrealistic foundations. In their eyes ideology is superior to human-beings who are the objects to digest the inhuman ideology. The result is that sooner or later the castle collapses, but the tragedy of human-beings lasts over decades. Earlier examples are experiments with Nazism and Communism. After the fall of Nazism, at least two generations of Germans suffered from the syndromes of that ideology. The Soviet-block countries and the Commonwealth of Independent States (ex-USSR countries) are currently passing through the consequences of the inhuman Communism. Now the post-Tálibán human catastrophe is in the horizon. All that a common person can do is to blame the Almighty for sending him to the Earth.

Every modern society is modest, educated and affluent economically, and does not even think of territorial gains by war. The days of old-fashioned war with artillery, bombs and guns are gone. At present the best weapon of a country is its solid economy, and industry is the backbone of a solid economy. Typical economic powers are: USA, Japan and Germany. We should remember that Japan is a tiny country made up numerous islands. Still Japanese economy competes with the economies of big countries like USA and Germany. All these big powers have one thing in common: economic ideology. Both Germany and Japan fought the second World War by conventional weaponry and lost it. Now they do not have to fight a war to gain territory. They have already the whole World won economically. Therefore, why should they die in wars? They came to the Earth to live and they live peacefully and happily.

What did go wrong with us? Two things went wrong. First, the State of Pákistán came into being as a result of artificial division based on religion. Second, after the partition the political leadership in both India and "United" Pákistan misled us and deceived us. Both the partition of British India and the dishonesty of "our leaders" accelerated the process of degeneration of the entire "nation." In British India the British ruled, but after the independence "Brown Sáhibs" substituted the out-going ruling elite in India while "Khán Sáhibs" grew to rule in Pákistán. This ruling clan not only demoralized common man but also resulted in further degeneration of the nation. The common man started suffocating in his own house and, depending on the degree of tolerance, started jumping out of the house walls, both legally and illegally.

Now some words about the partition of British India. The territories of India and Pákistán were demarcated on the basis of census records, and were supposed to be Hindu and Muslim states, respectively. From West Pákistán practically the entire Hindu and Sikh population either voluntarily migrated or was driven out to Independent India. In East Pákistán some percent of Hindus and Sikhs remained, but slowly they also started migrating to India under pressure of religious intolerance there. A large percent of Muslims, especially in Uttar Pradesh, Bihár, Madhya Pradesh, Gujarát, Kerala and Rájasthán, opted to remain in India. Now plus one-eighth of the population of India is Muslim. In contrast, rhetoric in Pákistán of Hindu India as a Big Demon, standing at the doorstep of Pákistán, has been continued vigorously unabated since 1947. I know of one Big Demon invented in Hitler by the Soviets after the Second World War. That Demon was a part of every official speech of leaders in the Soviet Union and most of the Soviet war films for 45 years. The Soviet citizens lived in an atmosphere of constant danger and uncertainty. It served nobody. On the contrary, the propaganda damaged the psyche of ordinary Soviet citizens. The approach in Pákistán has been exactly the same as that of the Soviets.

Since its creation Pákistán as a nation had the problem of identity. As the partition of British India was made on religion, the ruling elite in Pákistán started to develop an atmosphere of superiority in the minds of the citizens based on Islam and Muslim aristocracy of "non-Indian" origin, that ruled over pre-partition India. The vigorous propaganda indeed brought the desired results, but in the process Pákistán as a nation tried to forget the most important historical fact that its population and its territories were the other day parts of the same heritage, same culture and same roots. If the two countries were from the same land, then why the Pákistáni rulers and citizens tried to shed off the common roots. The reason is simple. They tried to portray their superiority complex by being Muslims, while the Kafirs of the pre- and post-partition India were not worthy of attention. The citizens of post-partition India had the psychological comfort of continuing to be Indians, while the citizens of the new state of Pákistán felt the problem of identity. They were Indians no more. Regretfully, they even remained adamant to admit that they shared a common past with the post-partition Indians.

In order to fill the gap of identity and to find common roots somewhere, Pákistán directed its attention to Islam and Islamic countries. For example, Pákistán's participation in the activities of the Organisation of Islamic Countries is remarkable. All that Pákistán could show were Islamic values nurtured in Pákistán, thinking that other Islamic countries were unaware of them. This was again based on: "We are superior Muslims to you Muslims" or "We know better." The crisis of identity had been severe in "West Pákistán", where every citizen considered himself as a direct descendent of the Nawábs that ruled some part of pre-partition India. They simply refused to accept that they were made from the same clay as the "káfirs" who remained behind in the post-partition India. In contrast to his countrymen from West Pákistán, in "East Pákistán" the common man remembered that he was a Bengáli and his cultural heritage and roots were the same as those of the "Indian Bengális." This was the main difference between East and West Pákistáni mindset. This false concept of superiority made the West Pákistánis arrogant, aggressive and uncompromising, all qualities that are required to alienate such people from the others. This was indeed the cause of secession of East Pákistán from the then united Pákistán and its emergence as Bangládesh.

It is strange that the ruling elite in Pákistán did not draw any conclusions from the separation of Bangládesh. They still remain ignorant of the simple fact that the population of Muslims in India is more than that in Pákistán. Instead, even after the emergence of Bangládesh they have continued intensively the policy of spreading hatred against India from the standpoint of theory of Hindu India and Muslim Pákistán. Every now and then there are voices raised in Pákistán about the fate of Muslims in India. This is an insult to the self-pride of Indian Muslims. They are certainly not made from a worse clay than the Pákistánis. After all, who made Pákistán a spokesman of Indian Muslims? Alternatively, if Pákistán does not want Muslims to live in India as Indians, it should spell out clearly whether it wants them to live in Pákistán. Looking to its economic resources and possibilities, this will be certainly another big adventure undertaken by the present-day Pákistán.

Now the roots of Pákistánis. To understand this, let us recall only two episodes of the history of India. First, the territory of the Present Pákistán covers the regions of Indus civilisation, which prospered on the banks of Indus river. Indus Civilisation dates back to 3000-4000 BC. The names of the Province "Sindh", the religion "Hindu", and the name of the country "India" or "Hindustán" are derived from the name of the "Indus" or " Sindhu" river. At that time there was no Islam, because Islam is just 1500 years old. Pákistán, on the other hand, has so far existed as an Islamic State only 54 years. Logically then one may ask: who lived in the territories of the present-day Pákistán? Pákistánis? No, they cannot be Pákistánis because they have lived as Pákistánis in the state of Pákistán only for 54 years. Muslims? Again no, Islam was not present at the time of Indus Civilisation some 5000-6000 years ago. Concerning the second episode, let us ask ourselves the question: who ruled India before the British? True, Muslims but where they came from. History tells that for a long period the Mughals ruled India. The first was Babur and the last one worth remembering was Aurangzeb. Babur was an Uzbek but all his descendants assimilated with the local kings through marriages. In general, with the exception of Aurangzeb, they showed religious tolerance. Hindus embraced Islam either to save their lives under the prevalent terror of rulers like Aurangzeb or to acquire privileges of becoming a part of the ruling elite willingly. The point is that except for a small number of soldiers who came with Babur, there was no mass migration of Muslims from outside. Ethnically, the present-day Muslims in Pákistán, Bangládesh and India are the same as their Hindu counterparts living in these countries. Not only have the Pákistánis and Bangládeshis the same facial appearance as the Indians, but they also have the same common culture and the same languages. It is strange to recollect that Mohammad Ali Jinnah and Mahátamá Gándhi talked in their mother-tongue Gujaráti during their conversations and Poet Iqbal's ancestors were Kashmiri Pandits. Iqbal's famous song "Sáre Jáhán se achchhá Hindustán hamárá" is a testimony of our common roots. Not only this, even the surnames of Muslims in Pákistán are the same as those of Hindus in India. Some examples are: Bhat, Bhandári, Sethi, Tarár, Sehgal, Bájwá, Bhatti, Sandhu, and Kanwal. It will not be a surprise if I find someone with my surname in the "Pious Land."

In Pákistán, attempts were made to erase the common cultural and historical past by erecting a sky-high wall in the name of religion on its borders to save the "Pious Land" from the "Land of Demons." The ruling elite forgot about the common man, who became an object for experimentation. This elite did exactly the same as the Soviets. Exported ideology and forgot about the basic principles of economy. Soviet Union collapsed but Pákistán is there. Still there are chances that everything becomes normal. The tension across the Indo-Pák border can also ease because essentially there is nothing worth a dispute. There are simply differences of opinion regarding the existence of the two states on religious ground. However, it is for the Pákistáni elite to understand that they are living in the twenty-first century. They have a neighbour much bigger in size and economically better than Pákistán. From the sheer strength of force or threat Pákistán cannot win. Pákistán has to accept that their neighbours, small or big, have the right to live as they want and not as Pákistán wants. And if there are disputes with another country, it should solve them amicably through dialogue. Willingness to compromise is required on both sides. The wall separating Pákistán from India is unwanted.

Since independence 54 years have passed. The countries of the entire Subcontinent (Pákistán, Bangládesh, Nepál, India, Bhután and Sri Lanká) have essentially the same problems. They are: population growth, poor education opportunities, poor economy, unemployment, women welfare, social injustice, corruption and poor public administration. These problems are huge and enormous. It is high time that the ruling elite in all these countries forgets about its superior (and inferior) complexes and rises above egoism and sentiments to solve the problems faced by the citizens. A state of permanent tension or war in these countries will never bring prosperity to them. If they cannot exist together as one country due to historical or religious reasons, and common heritage and culture, all of them can still live together by solving the common problems by removing the walls of hatred and complexes. Facilitate mutual contacts between their citizens and allow free trade to improve the economy. Other things will follow automatically. The ruling elite must think of the common man and stop doing experiments on him. Enough of these experiments. Why should the poor common man, whom the Almighty created with the same zeal and dedication, irrespective of his geographical location, language and religion, suffer from the political game of the ruling elite?

July 2002

GLOSSARY

a, á

Ardh Kumbh Mela held after 6 years at the site of Full Kumbh Mela, which is held every 12 years; ardh means half

ártee religious song usually sung in Hindu temples in morning and evening prayers in praise of a god/goddess

b

bahin sister

bájari millet-like grain grown in poor-quality land

beedee cigar-shaped rolled tobacco leaves with pointed ends for smoking in Indian sub-continent

beeghá measure of land equal to 0.625 acre

ben sister; a simple version of 'bahin'

bhajan religious song usually sung in religious gatherings and in temples

bhangrá a traditional folk dance of Punjab, associated with the Vaisakhi festival, marking the season of harvesting

bhábhee brother's wife; form of address to friend's wife or elder cousin's wife

bhái brother; elder brother when added at the end of a given name

c

chak measured rural fields or areas for agriculture as an inhabitable unit

cháchá uncle; father's younger brother; commonly used in Punjáb

chárpáyee easily moved cot for sitting and sleeping; literally four-legged

chowkee thigh-high elevation in or outside a building

d

darwázá roofed building composed of two high walls with
high gates

dhábá small restautant-like place to take traditional Indian
food and Indian-style tea

dhoti loin-cloth as customarily worn by male Hindus

Diwáli also called Deepawali, festival of lights, most celebrated festival in India, when houses, streets and shops
are decorated with beautiful lights

dopahariyá food taken at noon; literally associated with
two (do) three-hours (pahars)

Dussehrá an important Hindu festival, celebrating the
victory of good over evil, on the tenth day of the seventh
month of the Hindu calender, falling in September and
October

e

Ermitaż a museum of art and culture in Sankt Petersburg,
Russia, known as 'Hermitage Museum' in English

g

ghee clarified butter

garbá dance popular folk dance in Gujarát

German Democratic Republic popularly known as
East Germany, with the acronym GDR in English and
DDR in German

guláb-jámun a dessert made mainly from milk reduced
to the consistency of a soft dough

gurudwárá a place of worship for Sikhs; literally, gate to Guru

h

Habilitation degree a post-PhD degree something like DSc, called 'doktor habilitowany' in Polish, awarded to candidates based on his/her scientific achievements after PhD

Holi a popular Hindu festival celebrated as the Festival of Colours, Love and Spring

hooká tobacco pipe with a long flexible tube through which smoke is drawn through water in a vase

j

jutee regional brand of leather shoes

k

karhee a sour spicy soup prepared from skimmed milk and chick-pea flour

káká uncle, father's younger brother (declining use now but still commonly used in many parts of India); also used to address young boys in Punjabi-speaking families

khádi derived from khaddar, a hand-spun and woven natural fibre cloth promoted by Mahatma Gandhi

Kumbh Mela a major pilgrimage in Hinduism, celebrated every 12 years at different cites; mela held every 12 years is Pooran (Full) Kumbh mela, while the one held after 6 years at the same site is known as ardh (half) mela

kurtá shirt with short or without collars

l

Leningrad a city of the Soviet Union, known as Petrograd in Tsarist Russia and Sankt Petersburg in present Russian Federation

m

mela a gathering, a fair

magazin grocery store in the Soviet Union

MLA acronym for Member of Legislative Assembly in the States of India

p

patwári the lowest state functionary responsible for maintaining ownership records of land and plantation of crops in villages under his/her jurisdiction

plov central Asian dish of rice cooked with mutton and different spices; its cousins are Spanish paella and Indian puláw

r

rasgullá a popular Bengali dessert of soft round dumplings, made from cottage cheese and special wheat flour, simmered in a cardamom and rosewater scented sugar syrup

Rám-leelá deeds of Lord Rama

roti popular round flatbread made from whole wheat flour; also known as chapati in English

s

salwár-kameez a traditional dress for women combining a trouser (salwár), atypically wide at the waist and narrow to a cuffed bottom and a long shirt (kameez)

shrikhand a delicious and simple dessert made with thick yogurt flavored with sugar, saffron and cardamom

Simferopol a city in Crimea, Ukraine

subbotnik day of volunteer unpaid work on weekend; the name has its roots in the Russian word 'subbota' for 'Saturday'

Swamináráyan faith also known as Swaminarayan Hinduism and Swaminarayan movement, characterized by the worship of its charismatic founder Sahajanand Swami, better known as Swaminarayan (1781–1830), as an incarnation of Krishna and Vishnu

t

takiyá residence of a sádhu in the village

tandeer roughly cylindrical clay oven with narrowing top for baking loaves in Turkey, similar in shape and function to traditional tandoor of India

táluká see 'tehsil'

táyá big uncle; father's elder brother; commonly used in Punjáb

táyoo another spoken version of 'táyá', big uncle

tehsil traditional administrative unit in different States of India, also known as táluká in some States like Gujarát

thánedár head of basic police unit

tilak mark created by powder or paste on the forehead; a Hindu ritual

v

Vidyápeeth literally back or backbone (peeth) of knowledge (vidyá), officially considered lower than a University in the education system